Three Realms of Ethics

Individual
Institutional
Societal

Theoretical Model and Case Studies

John W. Glaser

Sheed & Ward

Sheed & Ward™ is a service of The National Catholic Reporter Publishing Company.

Library of Congress Cataloguing-in-Publication Data

Glaser, Jack.
    Three realms of ethics : individual, institutional, societal / John W. Glaser.
        p.   cm.
    Includes bibliographical references.
    ISBN 1-55612-722-7 (alk. paper)
    1. Medical ethics—Religious aspects—Christianity. 2. Christian
ethics. 3. Ethics. 4. Medical ethics—Case studies. I. Title.
    [DNLM: 1. Ethics, Medical—case studies. 2. Religion and Medicine.
3. Catholicism. W 50 G48t 1994]
R725.56.G58 1994
174'.2—dc20
DNLM/DLC
for Library of Congress   94-19442
                                               CIP

Published by: Sheed & Ward
                115 E. Armour Blvd.
                P.O. Box 419492
                Kansas City, MO 64141

To order, call: (800) 333-7373

Cover design by Emil Antonucci.

Contents

Part II
Case Studies

To the memory of my parents,
Clarence and Margaret Glaser,
and to our children,
Brian and Meg Glaser:
four of the best teachers of ethics
I have known.

Theoretical Model

Part I:
Theoretical Model

Introduction

Another map of ethics:

Imagine that someone handed you a AAA road map of California and suggested that this represented the state. If you want to drive from Santa Ana to Sacramento, the statement is a valid one. But if you want to drill for oil, plant a vineyard, sell medical supplies, or run for public office—a map of California highways is the wrong map. I am concerned that too often in healthcare ethics we have taken one of many valid maps and treated it as if it were the one, true map of ethics.

Ethics, like friendship, marriage, or death, for example, is too rich a reality to fit into any simple, single conceptualization. As Samuel Johnson reminded us: "We are moralists perpetually, geometers only by accident." So morality is as broad and deep as life itself. It demands a correspondingly wide range of mental models and paradigms.

Morality is as broad and deep as life itself. It demands a correspondingly wide range of mental models and paradigms.

A strength of recent criticisms of medical ethics is their thrust to expand our understanding of ethics to better approximate the scope of the reality. A weakness of some criticisms is that they give the impression that they have arrived with the true map. It seems obvious that the truth lies in no single map but in the complementarity of many essential maps. Perhaps we should all have a dozen or so favorite "maps"—several cartoons, a poem, a short story, half-a-dozen conceptual models, a parable—that capture for us the richness and variety of what ethics is about.

The following slim volume intends to offer another partial map of ethics. A map that has been helpful to me and to others with whom I have shared it. I have reached into the Catholic Christian tradition of ethics to construct this model, believing that this tradition has much to offer the larger ethical effort of our community—just as it has much to receive from this larger effort.

Understanding Ethics in Terms of Beneficence

I believe that a Christian tradition that considers beneficence as the center of the moral life has much to offer the current discussion of health care ethics. In much recent bioethical discussion "beneficence" is only one of several basic principles. But in a long-standing Christian tradition, beneficence stands as the foundational principle, grounding all else. I believe that this classic Christian perspective on the moral life can open some fresh vistas for the ethics of health care.

I will divide this book into four parts: 1) will develop a model of ethics that is beneficence-based; 2) will develop three spheres of beneficence: individual, institutional, societal, and will explain the differences that exist between these spheres; 3) will draw some conclusions from the first two sections; 4) will present a series of cases with questions and suggest ways to use them as tools of ethical reflection and education.

I. A Sketch of Ethics as Beneficence

Loving in the Situation of Finitude

We can begin our understanding ethics in terms of beneficence by considering a variation of the parable of the Good Samaritan.

The Conflicted Samaritan

A man was once on his way down from Jerusalem to Jericho and fell into the hands of brigands; they took all he had, beat him and then made off, leaving him half dead. Now a priest happened to be traveling down the same road, but when he saw the man, he passed by on the other side. In the same way a Levite who came to the place saw him, and passed by on the other side. But a Samaritan traveler who came upon him was moved with compassion when he saw him. He went up and bandaged his wounds, pouring oil and wine on them. He then lifted him on his own mount. As the Samaritan traveled further, he came upon another man who had been beaten and needed care. He likewise ministered to him and set him on his mount. As the three turned the next bend in the road, the Samaritan's heart sank for there were two more figures lying on the side of the road in the foreground and further, before the road turned in the distance, he made out one further traveler, struck to the ground and needing help. His heart was filled with pity and compassion—but with growing distress—for his resources would be exhausted long before he reached the last person in his view. And he could only guess at what lay around the next bend.

His resources would be exhausted long before he reached the last person in his view.

The struggle is between values each of which is an undoubted good in its place but which now get in each other's way.

This parable presents two kinds of ethical conflicts:

1) the *existential* ethical crisis of the priest, Levite, and Samaritan who confront their duty and make a decision. This volume will not concern itself with such ethical decisions; and

2) the *normative* ethical crisis where, in Dewey's terms, "The struggle is not between a good which is clear to him and something else

which attracts him but which he knows to be wrong. It is between values each of which is an undoubted good in its place but which now get in each other's way" ([14], p. 7).*

With this parable as a starting point, I will first develop the idea that all normative decisions represent such conflicting loyalties and that we have not taken sufficient note of this underlying values-in-conflict fabric of our ethical life.

Love of neighbor stands as the basic commandment of Christian morality. In *Quadragesimo Anno* Pius XI says: "all the commandments. . . may be reduced to the single precept of true charity" ([39] #137). In Christian Scripture the most dramatic and stark presentation of the central role of love of neighbor comes in Mt. 25, when religion and morality are cast in these surprisingly simple terms of response to neighbor's need:

All the commandments . . . may be reduced to the single precept of true charity.

> Then the King will say to those on his right hand, "Come, you whom my Father has blessed; take for your heritage the kingdom prepared for you since the foundation of the world. For I was hungry and you gave me food; I was thirsty and you gave me drink; I was a stranger and you made me welcome; naked and you clothed me, sick and you visited me, in prison and you came to see me. Then the virtuous will say to him in reply, "Lord, when did we see you hungry and feed you; or thirsty and give you drink? When did we see you a stranger and make you welcome; naked and clothe you; sick or in prison and go to see you? And the King will answer, "I tell you solemnly, in so far as you did this to one of the least of these brothers of mine, you did it to me." (Mt. 25: 34-40)

Karl Rahner has elaborated the theology behind this passage when he delineates the radical unity of love of God and love of neighbor [41, 42]. He poses the question: is love of neighbor identical with love of God to the radical extent that no act of love of God can occur which is not an act of neighbor-love? His short answer is, yes. A longer version says: "The primary act of love of God is the act of categorial-explicit love of neighbor. In this act of neighbor-love God is directly met in supernatural transcendentality—always unthematic but actually. The explicit act of love of God is always borne by this trusting, loving opening to all of reality which occurs in the act of love of neighbor. It is true with a radical—not merely psychological or 'moral'—necessity, that one who does not love one's brother, whom one 'sees,' cannot love God, whom one does not see, and that a person can only love God, whom one cannot see in so far as a person loves their visible neighbor" ([41], p. 295).

Persons can only love God, whom they cannot see, in so far as they love their visible neighbor.

If the commandment to love our neighbor is foundational, what of the other commandments—not to steal, kill, covet, and the like? How do they relate to this fundamental commandment? As species to genus. They

---

*Bracketed numbers refer to bibliographical listing, see pp. 39-41.

translate the foundational commandment of love into specific areas of life. Paul's letter to the Romans spells this out:

> If you love your fellow men, you have carried out your obligations. All the commandments: you shall not commit adultery, you shall not kill, you shall not steal, you shall not covet, and so on, are summed up in this single command: you must love your neighbor as yourself. Love is the one thing that cannot hurt your neighbor; that is why it is the answer to every one of the commandments. (Romans 13: 8-10)

Such passages have led systematic theologians such as Bruno Schüller to identify love as the foundation and love's structure as determinative of morality's method: "The double commandment of love of God and love of neighbor encompass the totality of moral claims that can be made on a person. Therefore, the manner of reasoning that serves to clarify this double commandment must be seen, in all cases, as fundamental" ([45], p. 527, [44-52]). Another Catholic theologian, R. Carpentier, identifies the essence of theological ethics to consist in articulating "the thousand-fold specific and concrete formulations of charity, the mother and root of all virtue" ([11], pp. 53-54). In carrying out this task of the thousand-fold specification of love, further distinctions are necessary.

Love as Benevolence – Beneficence

Catholic tradition has understood charity as comprised of two distinct but complementary and necessary elements: love as benevolence and love as beneficence. It is not enough to wish our neighbors well (*bene velle*), we must also act for their good (*bene facere*).

Beneficence is wholeheartedly directed to doing good but beneficence knows severest limits.

It is precisely this characteristic of wholehearted love, but love within limits, that sets a major agenda for an ethics of beneficence.

Charity is first and foremost *benevolence*—an attitude of the mind and heart that wishes the best for one's neighbor. Such an attitude is the heart of charity, the roots from which deeds of love spring. Love as benevolence is both comprehensive and universal. It wishes all good things to the neighbor and it recognizes the neighbor as everyone—including one's enemies. Benevolence knows no limits; it reaches, like God's love, from end to end with might and embraces all hearts with tenderness.

With *love as beneficence* things are leaner, more severe. Beneficence is wholeheartedly directed to doing good but beneficence knows severest limits: limits of knowledge, imagination, time, space, ability, resources. Essential to beneficence is its characteristic of love-within-limits. As Gustafson puts it: "the good is sought under the conditions of finitude" ([24], p. 141). *It is our nature as finite creatures, not a narrowness of heart, that fundamentally accounts for the limits of beneficence.* It is precisely this characteristic of wholehearted love, but love within limits, that sets a major agenda for an ethics of beneficence.

It is obvious that beneficence as understood in this way is essentially different from beneficence as it is commonly understood in the recent literature of bioethics. The latter understanding is much narrower than the former and is virtually synonymous with a paternalistic attitude toward patients. Pellegrino and Thomasma comment: "This is the conception of beneficence still dominant in the minds of many physicians and patients; it still shapes the ethos and ethics of medicine. It is the conception, too, that is the focus of criticisms by proponents of autonomy who equate beneficence almost entirely with medical paternalism" ([38], p. 13).

The understanding of our moral life proposed in this essay claims that we are always called to fulfill the basic commandment of love, of beneficence. And the nature of beneficence involves choosing between limited options. To illustrate this Schüller offers the example of a physician who stands in the situation where she can only provide a benefit to her patient by causing pain. Schüller then makes this point—a point foundational for our considerations here:

> In such a situation one stands before two values that compete with one another. To realize one value a person must leave the other unrealized. One must then decide which of the values deserves priority. If we look carefully we see here the characteristic and fundamental human condition: as a limited being, a person has only limited possibilities available for serving the neighbor's good. A person's actions cannot effectively benefit everyone, nor respond to any and every legitimate need and deficit. One must make a choice and decide which of those currently available possibilities deserves to be selected. One must, therefore, be able to choose between important and more important, between urgent and less urgent, between better, good and less good. This means that one must be able to grasp the preference imperative that prevails here amidst competing values. In our daily lives we are not normally conscious of this constant choosing between competing values. In any case, we have become so accustomed to this unrelenting value preference that it hardly ever catches our attention ([52], p. 70).

One must make a choice and decide which of those currently available possibilities deserves to be selected.

The moral imperative—the beneficence imperative—emerges from the weighing of human goods to be realized and evils to be avoided. Schüller makes two points central to our discussion: 1) this situation of facing and having to choose between conflicting values/disvalues constitutes the essential fabric of our moral life ("If we look carefully we see here the characteristic and fundamental human condition"); 2) we are usually unaware of this situation ("we have become so accustomed to this unrelenting value preference that it hardly ever catches our attention"). These two points parallel Max Weber's comment, cited by Schüller, that "all action . . . in its consequences boils down to partisanship on behalf of some values and—a fact so readily overlooked today—against other values" ([45], p. 532).

All action . . . in its consequences boils down to partisanship on behalf of some values and—a fact so readily overlooked today—against other values.

Beneficence: An Ethic of Values, Virtues, Character, Duties, Rights, Principles

What I have described in terms of beneficence can and should also be viewed from other partial perspectives and described in terms of values, virtues, character, duties, rights, loyalties, principles, etc. I want to take just one of these partial perspectives and summarize our discussion up to this point in terms of ethical principles.

In terms of ethical principles the architecture of such a beneficence ethics would be structured as follows:

1. Beneficence—not one of many coordinate principles but the foundational principle of which all else is specification. Such an ethics is grounded in benevolence—that attitude of heart that wishes well to all.

    1.1 Principle of proportionality—not one of many principles but the grounding instrumental principle which applies beneficence to specific situations. It can be referred to in other terms—as the principle of reasonableness, the best interest principle, or benefits-burdens principle.

    1.1.1., etc. All other principles—
    respect for life, respect for death,
    truth telling, respect for autonomy,
    informed consent, social justice, etc.—
    are principles with no preordained hierarchy; the priority must be established by ethical discernment in each specific situation.

That the fundamental situation of normative ethics always involves a choice for some values to the detriment of others has found various expressions across millennia and traditions.

Its cardinal importance has not been recognized and exploited for healthcare ethics.

Further, it would not be difficult to show the connections between a beneficence ethic and issues of virtue, character, and rights. Nor is it hard to imagine how casuistry or feminist ethics could relate to beneficence as developed above. But this is not the place for such further development.

An Overlooked Constant of Ethics

The insight that the fundamental situation of normative ethics always involves a choice for some values to the detriment of others has found various expressions across millennia and traditions. Cicero, Augustine, Aquinas, Max Weber, Lessing, Hartmann, Fichte, Ross, Thielicke, Dewey among others, speak to this issue. Still, in my opinion, its cardinal importance has not been recognized and exploited for healthcare ethics. This is puzzling, and deserves some exploration before we move on.

Prominent authors—rather than identifying values-in-conflict as an essential dimension of ethical existence—explicitly identify this as an occasional characteristic in ethical experience. For example, we read: "Sometimes we confront two or more *prima facie* duties or obligations, one of which we cannot fulfill without sacrificing the other(s)" ([12], p. 429). Another author says: "It is clear that an increasing number of theologians insist on understanding moral norms within the conflict model of human reality. Conflicted values mean that occasionally our choices (actions or omissions) are inextricably associated with evil. Thus we cannot always successfully defend professional secrets without deliberately deceiving others. . ." ([34], p. 75). If, as I am claiming, such value conflicts are omnipresent, how might one explain that this universal situation and its importance for ethics are so little noticed?

A partial explanation lies in Schüller's citation of Wittgenstein suggesting that "the aspects of things that are most important to us are concealed under their simplicity and their everyday nature. (One cannot notice the thing because it is always right in front of our eyes.)" ([50], p. 650). We can compare this to our breathing, to the structure of our mother tongue, to the rules of logic—we are inclined to notice these "infrastructures of life" only when they take the forms of aberrations or exaggerations. We only notice our breathing when we are "out of breath"; we spend weeks using our language without attending to its grammatical structure, until someone makes a grammatical mistake. The usual presence of these realities is an unthematic rhythm of life, remaining beneath the threshold of consciousness. Like the law of gravity, it is always present but rarely reflexively conscious.

The aspects of things that are most important to us are concealed under their simplicity and their everyday nature.

Then, too, most of the daily value conflicts are so disproportionate that their resolution is obvious and requires no explicit attention. Overlapping this consideration is the fact that macro life decisions—choice of profession, marriage, parenthood, and so forth—imply circles of subordinate micro-decisions that flow spontaneously from the priorities established in the macro-decision. Again, resolving the vast majority of our daily value conflicts takes place spontaneously and below the threshold of our attention.

Resolving the vast majority of our daily value conflicts takes place spontaneously and below the threshold of our attention.

Further, our language usage and mental paradigms habitually direct our attention away from rather than toward this value conflict dimension of life. I think of an experience I had recently which involved actions that could in certain circumstances qualify as: battery, sexual assault, invasion of privacy, infliction of bodily pain, causing anxiety, and inflicting financial loss. How did I refer to this experience in my conversations? As my annual physical exam. That is, I name this actual conflict of values in terms of the preferred value(s) that I judge to outweigh the disvalues involved. The same could be said of terms such as medication, hospitalization, inoculation, chemotherapy, surgery, X-ray, blood work, and so on, ad infinitum.

In this regard it is important to note how much language goes beyond being a mirror of life and functions as hammer and anvil of our conscious experience. Language shapes consciousness certainly as much as it reflects it. Werner Stark suggests that we recognize the role of language as a mental grid. "We see the broad and deep acres of history through a mental grid. . . . through a system of values which is established in our minds before we look out onto it—and it is this grid which decides . . . what will fall into our field of perception" ([53], pp. 16, 7-8).

The principle of double effect should be abolished and replaced by the principle of multiple effects that is present in all situations of ethical choice.

Sometimes it is our very ethical/philosophical efforts that do us the disservice of concealing this value-conflicting dimension of life. For example, the "principle of double effect" is part of the problem. The beneficence ethic elaborated above says: all normative issues involve actions with not only double but multiple effects. To single out—relatively rare—cases where "the principle of double effect" is applicable clearly implies that those other cases—the majority—do not have to be concerned about such conflicting value issues. The principle of double effect should be abolished and replaced by the principle of multiple effects that is present in all situations of ethical choice.

All medical care visits harms on patients: use of time, needle sticks, chemical insults, diminishment of money, and so forth.

Another example is the oft-repeated phrase from Hippocratic ethics: *primum non nocere*—first of all, do no harm. This phrase hides the basic operational mode of all medical intervention: doing harm because greater good is expected from it. As I pointed out above, all medical care visits harms on patients: use of time, needle sticks, chemical insults, diminishment of money, and so forth. Health care without harm is nonsense. The revealing rather than concealing formulation of the principle might read: *nocete secundum proportionem*—do harm to the extent that it is justified by the promise of greater good.

One of the major sources of hiding this aspect of all ethical choice is the unwarranted importance and attention given to the differences between teleology and deontology, and a corresponding neglect of the deeper and more fundamental problem that each of them must face: *how to resolve the conflicts that inevitably arise regardless of whether our basic focus is rules or actions, "duties" or "consequences."* Veatch refers to this when he says: "Utilitarians, formalists, and mixed formalists all have the problem of resolving competing ethical claims" ([57], p. 10).

Beyond this, the very terms "Christian charity" and "beneficence" diminish rather than heighten the awareness of conflict. Charity conjures up images of a state of frictionless harmony rather than a struggle with hard choices that result in some individuals and groups necessarily facing negative, possibly very harsh, consequences. Paul's words can lull us into the belief that hard choices are beyond charity: "Love is always patient and kind; it is never jealous; love is never boastful or conceited; it is never rude or selfish; it does not take offense, and is not resentful. Love takes no pleasure in other people's sins but delights in the truth; it is always ready to excuse, to trust, to hope, and to endure whatever comes." (1 Cor. 13, 4-7) Such a paean to love can easily create the impression that failures to accomplish this or that good must be the result of a deficient love. In fact, some failures to do good are precisely failures of beneficence. But such reality should not be allowed to mask a central truth of beneficence ethics: beneficence must always choose among competing goods to be accomplished, between competing evils to be avoided.

Also, ethics often speaks in a kind of voice—which Gustafson calls the "prophetic ethical voice" [24] and which Schüller—borrowing from Stoic philosophy—refers to as *Päranese* ([52], p. 14-40). This is a manner of ethical discourse that assumes that we know what should be done and gets on with the doing of what is good through encouragement, inspiration, warning. Virtually all New Testament ethics speak in this voice. In the words of Schreiner, such ethical discourse "arrives with penetrating force of expression, lacking all mitigating qualification, with a naked, honed edge of command. Its sentences are intended not as formulations for casuistic referral, but as clarions to startle attention" ([43], p. 19). Such an apodictic and prophetic voice operates much like the term "medical examination," as noted above. It points to a stage beyond normative discernment, where conflicts have been resolved and norms have been established. Mary Ann Glendon reminds us that as Americans we have a further cultural-linguistic handicap in perceiving such value conflict [22]. She argues extensively that as Americans we are addicted to court-oriented rights talk as a way of perceiving and talking about life. According to her, no other nation is so thoroughly addicted, nor does any other society define it in terms as fiercely adversarial, as ours. The result of this is an all-or-nothing, yes-no, win-lose mentality. Such patterns of thought, affect, and conversation tend to severely reduce the parameters of discussion, to emphasize the conclusion and its correctness, and to experience competing considerations not as counterbalancing and qualifying truths, but as error to be dismissed.

We might conclude this discussion with a visual representation of the ideas contained in the parable with which we began. The cartoon below captures the fabric of our lives as limited creatures called to beneficence— there is always more good calling to be realized than we have the capacity to accomplish.

Although we are always choosing between competing goods/values/ loyalties, we only become aware of this by way of the rarest exception.

There is always more good calling to be realized than we have the capacity to accomplish.

*Drawing by Mort Gerberg;© 1974
The New Yorker Magazine, Inc.*

Even a cursive list of considerations such as the above makes it understandable that although we are always choosing between competing goods/values/loyalties, we only become aware of this by way of the rarest exception. A primary task of an ethic of beneficence is to provide this conflictual dimension of beneficence and the key elements of its resolution the prominent place that they deserve.

II. Expanding the Concept of Beneficence

Concentric Circles of Individual, Institutional, and Societal Beneficence

The complexity of this is further compounded by the fact that we not only choose between conflicting goods concerning individuals—as both the parable and the cartoon could lead us to believe—but also within and between concentric realms of values/goods/loyalties: the individual realm, the organizational realm, and the societal realm.

In this section I want to develop a model for understanding beneficence/ethics in terms of three interdependent but different realms: individual, institutional, and societal. I have found this model helpful in the conceptual exploration and practical implementation of many ethical concerns.

Our current language and paradigms often mask the unity and diversity of these realms. Those of us with our roots in U.S. culture and traditional Christian piety tend to bring a strong proclivity for individualism to moral concerns [3, 4, 8, 22, 27, 30, 31]. We tend to see the individual level as the home of authentic ethics with other concerns as weak analogues.

The New Testament (though it need not) more often inhibits than facilitates an expanded vision. The key Christian parables of healing deal with interactions between individuals. The parable of the Good Samaritan—a towering paradigm for Chrstians involved in healing ministries—stamps our imagination with images of individuals responding or not to another individual. The classic Christian description of love in 1 Corinthians also fastens our gaze on individual beneficence: "Love is patient; love is kind. Love is not jealous, it does not put on airs, it is not snobbish. Love is never rude, it is not self-seeking, it is not prone to anger; neither does it brood over injuries. Love does not rejoice in what is wrong but rejoices with the truth. There is no limit to love's forbearance, to its trust, its hope, its power to endure." With such powerful gravitational pull to keep our cognitional, imaginative, and affective dimensions firmly planted on the turf of individual beneficence, flight to higher realms of beneficence will take serious and systematic effort.

But there are sources of help. Roman Catholic thought has long distinguished between individual morality and social morality, although the language is not always consistent and its actual application is often confused and spotty. Still, this tradition offers a singularly helpful starting point with its *distinction between individual and social morality.* The U. S. Catholic bishops say: "Christians believe that Jesus' commandment to love one's neighbor should extend beyond individual relationships to infuse and transform all human relations from the family to the entire human community. . . . Such action necessarily involves the institutions and structures of society, the economy and politics" ([55], p. 732). These thoughts have their theological precedents and parallels in the writings of Catholic theologians such as Maritain [36], Murray [37], Curran [13], and McCormick [35].

Maritain understands politics as a branch of ethics. He distinguishes between political ethics and individual ethics ([36], 62-63). John Courtney Murray provided the Second Vatican Council with effective tools for developing a new understanding of religious liberty by emphasizing the "analogical character of the structures of life (personal, familial, political, social)" ([37], 290). "It follows, then, that the morality proper to the life and action of society and the state is not univocally the morality of personal life, or even of familial life. Therefore the effort to bring the organized action of politics and the practical art of statecraft directly under the control of Christian values that govern personal and familial life is inherently fallacious. It makes wreckage not only of public policy but also of morality itself" ([37], 286).

We have here a clear recognition of the difference between individual and what I have called societal realms of morality. What we do not have, either in the broader Catholic community nor in the world of biomedical discourse, is: 1) a more detailed conceptual development of these realms, their constituent parts, and the relationships that exist between these different realms; 2) a broad consensus on this point. A good example of both the strengths and weaknesses of the present situation is an article by Charles Curran where he makes a clear case for the difference between individual and societal ethics, but lacks a conceptual consistency, using the following pairs interchangeably: personal morality and public policy; realm of morality and realm of legality; legal order and moral order; private morality and public policy; individual and political morality; political and individual ethics ([13], 194-202).

With the following model I want to take this fundamental insight of Christian tradition that distinguishes between individual and social ethics and specify it further. Schematically we can imagine a model of beneficence along the lines sketched on the next page.

Jesus' commandment to love one's neighbor should extend beyond individual relationships to infuse and transform all human relations from the family to the entire human community.

The morality proper to the life and action of society and the state is not univocally the morality of personal life, or even of familial life.

Realms of Beneficence/Ethics

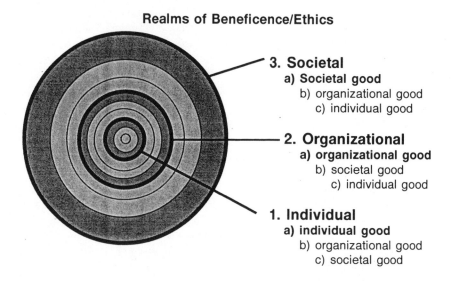

3. Societal
a) **Societal good**
b) organizational good
c) individual good

2. Organizational
a) **organizational good**
b) societal good
c) individual good

1. Individual
a) **individual good**
b) organizational good
c) societal good

Individual Beneficence

The simplest realm of beneficence/ethics is the realm of individual beneficence. Here the concern is primarily with the good of individuals. This concerns individuals and their relationships: the relationships that exist within one individual between various values and needs—physical, emotional, mental, and spiritual. It also attends to differences in degree and intensity within and between these goods—for example, it must weigh the relative importance of intense physical good and moderate spiritual good. It attends to differences of probability and certainty, for example, between near certain emotional harm of a moderate degree and probable intellectual benefit to an extensive degree. It must attend to the whole range of comparable elements such as long/short term, partial/total, transient/abiding, direct/indirect, central/peripheral.

We are comparing apples and oranges—all the time; and, there is no simple, math-like formula for weighing and balancing such "non-comparables."

This realm also deals with weighing and balancing the values/goods/loyalties that stand in tension between two or more individuals. For example, we must weigh my privacy and your need to have information about me, or the need of one person to be treated and the danger of infection for the professional providing treatment. Again the issues of probability, long/short term trade-offs, degree and extent of harms and benefits all come into play.

Two issues are immediately evident: we are comparing apples and oranges—*all the time;* and, there is no simple, math-like formula for weighing and balancing such "non-comparables." We can only marshal all the human powers of discernment—reason, intuition, imagination, affect, humor—gifts of individuals and the synergy of community, discipline and surprise, method and madness to give ourselves the best chance to make such prudential judgments with consistency.

The first two decades of bioethics have dealt extensively with this realm of 1a. Most of this era's burning questions fit comfortably in this realm of individual good: patient autonomy, informed consent, privacy, patient rights, truth-telling, and confidentiality.

But beyond the intra- and inter-individual issues are questions that treat sphere 1b): relationships of individuals to organizations. What responsibilities do patients, nurses, physicians have to their hospital? What trade-offs in income, safety, efficacy of treatment, and confidentiality can individuals be expected to make for the benefit of the institution?

Beyond this realm are issues in the sphere of 1c): relationships of individuals to the common good of society. What personal benefits should I forego or burdens should I bear in order to make community benefits available or harms avoidable? For example, what limits on care, what delays or diminished quality should an individual accept in order that the whole community can be assured of basic services?

So, in this realm of individual beneficence/ethics there are three subperspectives: a) within and between individuals; b) from individuals toward organizations; c) from individuals toward the larger society.

Organizational Beneficence

Normally, the use of the word beneficence has only individuals as its referent. The present analysis understands beneficence in terms of organizations as well. Organizations are both subject and object of beneficence.

Organizations are both subject and object of beneficence.

The social realities that I refer to as "organizations"—a family, a union, a business, a hospital, a religious community—have an identity, a purpose, a history and character. They have vital systems which account for their vigor and health. They have commitments, claims, relationships, and responsibilities.

A primary object of organizational beneficence is the net organizational good—that is, a state of organizational vigor and development that enables the organization to maximize its purpose now and into the future. Each organization has its seat of responsibility—parents in a family, officials in a religious community, governance and management in a hospital. They must seek the net good of the organization just as individuals seek net good at an individual level. But obviously the resolution of beneficence choices, in terms of complexity and extent, increases exponentially at this level.

A primary object of organizational beneficence is the net organizational good.

But such pursuit of the organizational good must also consider: 2c) the individual good of those within the organization. For example, let us assume a demonstrated need for the good of a hospital to reduce its size. There are usually many ways to accomplish such a goal. The imperative of beneficence is to find the complex balance of burden/benefit distribution that serves organizational net good, but also attends to the needs of individuals. At what point, if any, does this kind and this intensity of individual need outweigh that kind and that intensity of organizational need? Does the sheer number of individuals involved—and if so, how many—shift the balance in weighing alternatives?

Organizational beneficence must also attend to 2b), the common good of the society within which the organization exists. For health care institutions not only provide health services, they are also a powerful cultural force and agent. By their presence, their promotional efforts, their budgets and their services health care institutions have a significant influence on what the general population thinks, hopes and demands in terms of health care. Hospitals not only respond to but also create demand in the general public about what to expect of a hospital by way of service, convenience, and opulence. Hospitals shape voter apathy, energy, and indignation—subtly but powerfully. In an over-bedded community a hospital could even have to face the subordination of its institutional good to the good of the community, resulting in its consolidation with another institution or even its dissolution.

Beneficence in the sphere of 2b) sustains a consciousness of the organization's impact on the larger society and insists that as the organization pursues its own net good, it do so constrained by this consideration: how can we best achieve the net good of the organization while also promoting the common good of society?

How can we best achieve the net good of the organization while also promoting the common good of society?

In daily operations these issues of organizational/institutional ethics are commonly thought of as "operational questions," "organizational issues," "financial concerns," "management issues," or "marketing programs." They are that. But in the terms of our discussion they must also be identified as central issues of organizational beneficence and, therefore, vital issues of ethics.

Societal Beneficence

The final realm of an ethic of beneficence is that of society. This realm deals with the common good of society. The *Hastings Center Report* defines the common good as "that which constitutes the well-being of the community—its safety, the integrity of its basic institutions and practices, the preservation of its core values. It also refers to the telos or end toward which the members of the community cooperatively strive—the 'good life,' human flourishing, and moral development" ([27], 6, [5]). Garrett Hardin offers a helpful illustration of the common good and how it differs and even conflicts with the good of individuals. He asks us to think of a group of herdsmen who share a common grazing pasture. As long as there is enough pasture to feed the cattle and rejuvenate itself for the future, each individual herder can pursue personal aggrandizement without jeopardizing the common good. But at some point the danger of overgraz-

Common good is that which constitutes the well-being of the community— its safety, the integrity of its basic institutions and practices, the preservation of its core values.

ing emerges if each individual continues to increase the size of his herd. As long as the horizon of reflection remains individual—"what benefit comes to me from adding one more animal to my herd?"—the problem can neither be identified in a timely way nor resolved. Hardin says: "Therein is the tragedy. Each man is locked into a system that compels him to increase his herd without limits—in a world that is limited. Ruin is the destination toward which all men rush, each pursuing his own best interest in a society that believes in the freedom of the commons. Freedom in a commons brings ruin to all" ([25], 1224).

Societal beneficence is another term for the ethics of the commons. It knows that the common good is not achieved by some invisible hand as we each pursue our own individual good. Societal beneficence brings heart, mind, imagination and hands to the nurturing of this common good.

Attending to the commons involves balancing the many conflicting needs/goods of the commons—education, housing, defense, health care, art, infrastructure, and so forth. Being unable to meet any one or all of these societal needs fully, we seek a reasonable balance among them. The major task of societal beneficence is continually to attend to this balance by correcting historical aberrations, adjusting to new forces and circumstances, and creating new opportunities so that society can be humane and nurture growth.

Being unable to meet any one or all of these societal needs fully, we seek a reasonable balance among them.

A further dimension of societal ethics concerns the balance within each sector of the common good—education, health, housing, and so forth. For example, achieving the "healthcare good" of society involves finding the appropriate balance among competing healthcare needs such as prevention and cure, acute and chronic care, research and education, administration and direct service.

The primary goal of societal ethics is not to attend to the unique and specific goals of each individual but to so structure society and allocate resources that the fabric of society in which individuals and institutions exist can be an environment of human flourishing. But in seeking this common good of society, the good of individuals and the good of organizations cannot simply be ignored. As in the other two realms of beneficence the concern must look in three directions: 3a) primarily to the common good, to the net good of society as a whole; 3b) secondarily to the good of organizations, and: 3c) the good of individuals.

The Circles of Beneficence as Applied to Euthanasia

By way of summary I want to take the question of euthanasia and sketch some of the issues that are raised on these three different levels of ethical importance.

By way of summary I want to take the question of euthanasia and sketch some of the issues that are raised on these three different levels of ethical importance.

Euthanasia as an Issue of Individual Ethics

On this level we struggle with questions such as the following: May I deliberately and actively end my own life? If yes, what justifying grounds do I need? Does my autonomous wish suffice? Do I need to be suffering unremitting pain? Must I have a terminal condition? Does only God have such ultimate dominion over dying or does God share this dominion with me? Is there an ethically significant difference between my refusing life-sustaining treatment and my taking a lethal dose of medication? Beyond having a right to end my life, do I have a duty to end my life under some circumstances? What would they be? Do you have a duty to prevent me from taking my life? Always? If not always, under what circumstances? Do you have a duty to help me take my life if I am unable to do it without your help?

We should establish the *definitions and distinctions* needed for this level. We need to decide to what extent the following is an adequate definition of euthanasia, and if it is not, what needs to be expanded: "a phrase sometimes used to describe the situation in which someone (perhaps a physician) administers some lethal agent, e.g., a bolus of air, potassium chloride IV, excessive barbiturates, with the intention of causing the cessation of organic functions necessary to life" ([28],125-6). This deliberate act of ending life might be distinguished from decisions to limit treatment—either by withholding or withdrawing—and thereby hastening death. One would decide whether it is helpful to use terms such as active and passive euthanasia or to distinguish between killing and allowing to die. Here one needs to face the fact that all descriptions have language of moral connotation—e.g., is this physician-assisted dying? physician killing? tolerated murder? assisted suicide? my final act of self-determination? or what? There is a considerable range of such definitional questions to be dealt with here.

Beyond these definitional issues one must also elaborate the complexity of principles, value priorities, paradigms, cases, decisional authority, and methodology. When we have resolved such questions on the individual level we know under what circumstances, if any, you or I may deliberately end the life of another person. To the extent that we arrive at clarity on these questions we have won a valuable prize of ethical effort. But it is decisive only on the level of individual ethics; it does not deliver any necessary conclusions for the higher and more complex levels of institutional and societal levels of the ethics of euthanasia. We need to work through each of these realms on their own.

When we have resolved such questions on the individual level we know under what circumstances, if any, you or I may deliberately end the life of another person.

Euthanasia as an Issue of Societal Ethics

In most discussions of euthanasia the societal dimension emerges as a secondary issue. The consideration starts with a focus on the individual, and the conceptual and affective center of gravity remains on this individual level. The progression of thought follows this line: a person in the final and punishing stages of disease is presented. The degree of pain and suffering is extreme; the patient experiences this condition as degrading and inhumane and requests that his/her life be ended. The case is then made that in such extreme circumstances patients surely have a right to prefer death over unmitigated suffering and they deserve our presence and assistance in ending their lives. Since present legal limits treat such assistance as homicide and put at risk of prosecution anyone who would assist the pleading sufferer, such laws should be changed. But the laws should be so crafted that they severely limit the possibilities of mistakes and/or abuse.

In such a line of argument societal considerations flow from and serve assumptions and conclusions made on the individual level. It is not uncommon to characterize such secondary societal questions as "slippery slope" concerns or questions of preventing abuse. An example of this basic approach is the article by Timothy Quill and Christine Cassel, "Care of the Hopelessly Ill: Proposed Clinical Criteria for Physician-Assisted Suicide" [40].

But the proposed paradigm of three-leveled beneficence suggests a different approach to euthanasia as a societal issue. Its central concern is this: *what arrangements promise the most humane situation of living, aging, and dying for our children and further future generations?* The complexity and extent of this examination is vast, but nothing less will do justice to the situation when our society defines the meaning of, authority over, and attitudes toward our final human mystery—death.

The following remarks point to a few of the key points essential to such a vast examination. They do not pretend to explore even these limited points adequately.

Societal ethics demands some *societal definitions of euthanasia*. Just as we tried to clarify on the individual level what euthanasia is and is not, so we need to take a similar step on the societal level. The definitional task on this level is virtually unexplored and exponentially more difficult. However, attempts at societal definition of the legalization of euthanasia might include the following:

- Societal establishment of the right of individuals to end their lives;

- Extension of patient autonomy to include physician-assisted death;

- Empowerment of patients to choose their time and circumstances of death;

- Privatization of some homicides: shifting a class of killings from being a matter for public scrutiny to being a matter of physician-patient privacy;

What arrangements promise the most humane situation of living, aging, and dying for our children and further future generations?

Societal ethics demands some societal definitions of euthanasia.

- Establishment of a new level of empowerment for physicians over the dying of their patients;
- Further medicalization of death and dying;
- Establishment of death as an event to be increasingly managed and planned by future generations;
- Introduction of the elements leading to a perceived duty to end one's life;
- Providing legal protection for those who provide legal aid in dying.

What can we say about such a suggestive and inadequate attempt to define euthanasia as a societal reality? First, many more definitions are needed on this level than on the individual level—no single definition can hope to capture the fullness of this societal reality. Next, there are few standard sources offering such societal definitions. Virtually all standard treatments of euthanasia define it in terms appropriate to the individual ethical realm and make no attempt to define it as a social reality. Further, it is extremely difficult to develop fair and objective societal definitions. Such societal definitions are much more susceptible to the smuggling in of one's ethical conclusions than is the case with definitions on the individual level. Also, no single discipline has a privileged vantage point from which to define the societal reality. Each discipline brings its sharper vision for some aspects of the issue, but this acuity is inevitably accompanied by a distance and alienation from other major dimensions of the reality. Further, where do you stop? Which of these societal dimensions are so essential that they must be included in an adequate societal definition and which are marginal enough to be excluded? Who decides these and similar central questions?

A serious approach to the societal ethics of euthanasia must include this struggle to elaborate definitions of euthanasia as a societal reality.

However inadequate these attempts at defining euthanasia as a societal reality, the task is as necessary as it is unaccustomed and difficult. A serious approach to the societal ethics of euthanasia must include this struggle to *elaborate definitions of euthanasia as a societal reality.*

Another stage in societal ethics involves attending to relevant *principles, assumptions and priorities.* For example, in a beneficence ethic, the foundational "beneficence principle" remains the same on all levels: *facing a situation in which we cannot realize all the values involved to the extent that we would wish, we must choose that option that best realizes the significant values at stake.* All other principles are tools to serve this one. They focus the community's awareness, exploration, discussions, and decisions. There is an enormous range of such subordinate principles, priorities, and assumptions. The following brief selection suggests a few such secondary/tertiary elements that need to be clarified and established in resolving the societal dimensions of euthanasia.

- When we significantly change expectations, understandings, attitudes, and behaviors about central mysteries of human existence—freedom, birth, sexuality, death, etc.—we are setting in motion a powerful and long-enduring *evolutionary process*, not merely making discrete and definable change in the immediate future.

- Social forces prevail over intended purposes: If the intention is to empower patients in their final decisions about care while the actual decision-making results more from physician preferences than from patient preferences, then we must expect the legalization of euthanasia to result more in the empowerment of physicians than of patients. This point has been made by critics of the euthanasia phenomenon in the Netherlands.

- An iron law of common good solutions is that some individuals must always sacrifice their own personal interests to the community's best interest. So, no resolution is disqualified simply because some individuals can be shown to be disadvantaged by this arrangement. The question of disadvantaged individuals boils down to this: which alternative results in less serious disadvantage for fewer individuals while fostering society's good?

- Social systems tend to perpetuate themselves even when they prove manifestly dysfunctional. So, here as elsewhere, prevention and cautious preparation has priority over rushed solutions.

An iron law of common good solutions is that some individuals must always sacrifice their own personal interests to the community's best interest.

Societal ethics must generate an adequate range of societal options and should rarely accept simple either-or scenarios. Even on the individual level, a simple "shall we do A or B?" is often a failing against moral imagination. But on the societal level a hasty narrowing of options can be catastrophic. Let us consider a range of options that address the problems for which euthanasia is often proposed as *the* solution.

Before legalizing physician-assisted death, we could intervene societally with varying degrees of coercion by:

- developing standards of practice that reduce patient overtreatment;
- requiring that health professionals demonstrate high levels of competency in managing pain and build this into professional education, licensure, board certification, etc;
- establishing required levels of competency in discussing death and dying with patients and in providing care appropriate for dying persons;
- educating and empowering the public so that they will not tolerate the poor management of pain and inappropriate care of the dying that is so widely practiced;
- developing an understanding of good and bad death and standards of care that promote good death.

A society intent on changing its legal prohibition of euthanasia has a wide range of options that vary greatly in their risk-benefit ratio for that society's future.

A society intent on changing its legal prohibition of euthanasia has a wide range of options that vary greatly in their risk-benefit ratio for that society's future. Some of these options include:

- imitating the Netherlands, where euthanasia remains a crime but is not prosecuted so long as specific guidelines are followed;

- maintaining euthanasia's status as a crime but accepting the legal defense of mercy;

- allowing only those physicians to practice euthanasia who have earned specific certification requiring demonstrated skills in communication and care of the dying;

- allowing the practice of euthanasia only by those physicians who are part of a licensed "terminal care team" which includes psychological, spiritual, and social professional competencies;

- allowing only assisted suicide, but not physician-administered death to treat the legalization of euthanasia as a social experiment with stringent design, data gathering, practice and evaluation requirements to be assessed in 2-3 years;

- instituting euthanasia IRB's that must approve each individual case prospectively, or review each case retrospectively;

- requiring a three-year environmental impact study to be submitted before any changes could be made.

Societal ethics requires that we spend extensive energy in generating options that go beyond the simplistic quick-fix.

It seems clear to me that many of the above options provide a better mix of societal risk and benefit than the usual proposal of moving euthanasia from felony to DRG. A serious and sustained examination of such options would help uncover vital aspects of legalizing euthanasia that would remain hidden if the only serious question is: shall we legalize physician-assisted death? Societal ethics requires that we spend extensive energy in generating options that go beyond the simplistic quick-fix.

We tend to fixate on the individual level of ethical reality while the problems confronting us are increasingly those of institutions and society.

These brief comments on euthanasia as an issue of societal ethics are meant only to touch some key areas that demand attention. But even this cursory look makes clear why I believe that societal ethics is a substantively and strikingly different enterprise than individual ethics. This presents us with an urgent challenge because culturally—generally in our U. S. culture and specifically in the subculture of U. S. healthcare—we tend to fixate on the individual level of ethical reality while the problems confronting us are increasingly those of institutions and society. Mary Ann Glendon's comment is apropos: "Our simplistic rights talk regularly promotes the short-run over the long-term, sporadic crisis intervention over systemic preventive measures, and particular interests over the common good. It is just not up to the job of dealing with the types of problems that presently confront liberal, pluralistic, modern societies" ([22], 15).

Euthanasia as an Issue of Institutional Ethics

I will take a hospital as my institutional referent for the following comments. For a hospital, what are some critical issues concerning the legalization of euthanasia?

To begin with, will this issue even cross the threshold of organizational consciousness and conscience? Will we explore the issue or ignore it? Will it become an object of our attention and investment when it becomes a political issue—a Proposition 161—or will we identify it as relevant now? Or will we see it as peripheral to our concerns, even when it is on our ballot? Do we see this primarily as a symptom of the inadequate care that hospitals provide dying patients or a more specific issue of patient autonomy?

A hospital could decide to be inactive about the issue of euthanasia for many reasons: because it has no clear institutional conscience on the issue; because it has a strong negative judgment but cannot justify expending any resources on the questions; because it favors legalizing euthanasia but considers its mission to be narrowly focused on the provision of health care under present societal definitions. Or an institution could be very active about euthanasia in a variety of ways: it could invest in broad, nonpartisan educational efforts for staff, patients, and community; it could strongly support the legalization of euthanasia through education and advocacy; it could take the stand that the best way to deal with requests for death is preventively and indirectly—for example, to aggressively deal with issues of pain management and appropriate treatment of the dying—in hospitals, long-term care facilities, and at home.

In arriving at its positions on these and many other aspects of the euthanasia question, the hospital would engage in much the same set of issues sketched for individual and societal challenges. It would need to clarify the conceptual, definitional issues. It would need to establish the principles/priorities of its discernment. It would identify the parties responsible for engaging in the exploration and decision and provide the processes appropriate for the breadth and complexity of the issues involved.

Determining the Primary Level of Ethical Concern

Most issues have ethical significance on all three levels and need to be addressed on each level appropriately. For example, informed consent has ethical concerns on the levels of individual, institution, and society. This issue deserves ethical inquiry. On the individual level, what should this physician disclose to this patient/family in this set of circumstances? On the institutional level, what policies, procedures, educational programs, patient brochures, quality assurance mechanisms, ethics committee activities should a hospital have to promote informed consent in the institution?

Most issues have ethical significance on all three levels and need to be addressed on each level appropriately.

On the societal level, what professional standards, federal regulations, state laws should be in place to promote a general practice of informed consent?

But hardly ever are these levels of equal importance. Some questions are primarily "institutional questions," with the individual/societal levels being secondary and/or tertiary considerations. Other issues are primarily issues of individual ethics, and still others are essentially issues of societal ethics.

For example, the decision to downsize an institution is primarily a question of *institutional ethics*. This means that the decision results from a careful examination and weighing of the good of the institution: for the good of the institution, is this drastic step necessary? What other alternatives must be tried? For how long? How should it be done? What follow-up is required for those terminated and the survivors? So, even though many individuals will suffer harm from such a decision, it can be the institution's responsibility to move forward with such a decision—for the good of the institution.

But the question of participation in an experimental treatment is primarily a question on the *individual level*. This question should be resolved in terms of the individual patient's best interest, as defined by the patient. One cannot justify forcing patient participation because the hospital's experimental program will greatly benefit, or because future generations will benefit. Those are considerations that an individual could include in their calculus on the individual level but could never justify an institution's coercive action.

The question of national health policy is an ethical issue on the *societal level*. For the sake of the common good of the United States many institutions—e.g., insurance companies, hospitals, universities—and many individuals—e.g., patients and clinicians—will have to accept serious burdens and limits set to their expectations and practices in order for society to create a reasonable and just health care system.

One of the fundamental starting points for ethical discussion will be to determine which level, if any, is the preeminent level of ethical importance. This presents us with a set of ethical questions that we seldom ask explicitly and clearly in current discussions. For example, in the extensive discussion of California's Proposition 161 (the proposition that would have authorized active euthanasia and physician-assisted suicide), most discussions went forward as if this were primarily an issue of individual ethics with some secondary questions on the societal level—primarily formulated in terms of prevention of abuse. There would have been a different series of discussions had we all presumed that Prop 161 was essentially a question of societal ethics—or even if we had begun by asking which level deserved to be primary.

How does one establish the preeminent level? While the fullness of this consideration can only emerge from the community addressing these difficult questions over time, the following suggestions are an invitation to

One of the fundamental starting points for ethical discussion will be to determine which level, if any, is the preeminent level of ethical importance.

There would have been a different series of discussions had we all presumed that Prop 161 was essentially a question of societal ethics.

take up this challenge. I will phrase these in terms of ethical presumptions (I cast these in terms of *societal* ethics, but with appropriate changes, similar presumptions could be formulated concerning individual and institutional ethics).

A question is presumed to be one of societal ethics if

- it has serious consequences for future generations;
- it involves interdependence of major societal institutions—political, economic, educational, legal, etc.;
- it demands sacrifices from significant numbers on behalf of others;
- it has disproportionate impact on identifiable groups of persons;
- it requires extensive studies of multiple disciplines to reasonably represent its complexity;
- it has impact on significant institutions—schools, businesses, groups of professionals, etc.;
- it requires organization and integration of such complexity that individuals and institutions cannot accomplish it adequately;
- it endangers the already marginalized;
- it involves long-standing cultural assumptions;
- its center concerns pivotal mysteries of life—sexuality, partnering, aging, dying, etc.
- its success requires broad, coercive measures.

A question is presumed to be one of societal ethics if its success requires broad, coercive measures.

Such modest suggestions invite critique and modification; they point to a body of ethical thought that should rank high on the list of priorities for the future.

Summary

Mapping Ethics as Love

Mapping ethics as love conceives the heart of human existence as the invitation, opportunity, and duty to care for ourselves and one another in the boundless realm of our minds and hearts (benevolence) and in the limited realm of our actions (beneficence). Because our acts of beneficence are always choices among competing values, goods, claims in three realms —individual, organizational, and societal—we need to construct a system of assistance, a grammar or logic which helps us apply beneficence to the thousands of unpredictable situations we will meet. This "logic of caring" is the discipline of ethics. As Maguire says: "To be moral is to love well. How to love well amid conflicting claims is the problem. Love needs a strategy and that strategy is ethics" ([29], 110).

To be moral is to love well. How to love well amid conflicting claims is the problem. Love needs a strategy and that strategy is ethics.

Unity and Diversity of Beneficence Across the Three Realms

Unity:

First, it is important to emphasize the fundamental unity of benefi-cence/ethics across these spheres. The emphasis on such unity and the interdependence of these spheres on one another is a major strength of the model developed above. Too often our language masks this unity instead of emphasizing it. Authors distinguish "morality" from "public policy," the "abstract order of ethics" from the "concrete order of jurisprudence," the "moral order" from "public policy" [5, 13, 15, 23, 35]. Such distinctions can be valid, but they should be the subtext, not the text. We need to develop a conceptual world and language that first emphasizes the unity of morality as we move across these spheres. Absent this foundation, we reinforce the common error that the "authentic world of ethics" resides in the realm of individual good and that beyond such real ethics lies only the ethical "outback" of politics, common sense, and law. We further make the mistake of approaching all ethical questions with the conceptual tools, moral imagination, and methodology adequate only for the simplest level of ethical reflection. Such misperception blunts our awareness of the most demanding areas of ethics, and tends to fragment our moral intellect and imagination. A major strength of this paradigm resides in its emphasis on the unity of ethical reality.

We need to develop a conceptual world and language that first emphasizes the unity of morality as we move across these spheres.

Diversity:

But beneficence/ethics across these realms is analogous, not univocal, and this involves significant differences between these spheres with relationships of interdependence that are not always parallel or reciprocal in every way. A brief sketch of some differences would include the following:

Ethics across these realms is analogous, not univocal, and this involves significant differences between these spheres.

1. All things being equal, as we move from realm 1 to 3, the ethical reality becomes exponentially both more significant and more complex;

2. Methods, concepts, and principles are presumed not to have the same importance, relevance, and adequacy on one level as they do on another. (For example: The principle of autonomy has an importance on level 1a that it does not sustain on level 2a, and is relativized still more on level 3a.);

3. Conclusions reached on one level do not lead to necessary conclusions on another level. (For example: To demonstrate that active euthanasia could be an ethically reasonable option in an individual case does not lead with any logical necessity to substantive conclusions on the organizational level and even less so on the societal level);

Conclusions reached on one level do not lead to necessary conclusions on another level.

4. Substantial deficits on a higher level cannot be adequately compensated for by interventions on a lower level. (For example: It is not possible to correct a substantially unjust health care system merely by multiplying the activity of individual hospitals or health professionals);

5. The ethical character of the higher spheres tends to powerfully define the limits on ethical behavior in the sphere(s) below. (For example: The injustices of a societal system—e.g., Medicaid—will tend to inhibit just behavior of institutions and professionals by punishing those who attempt to behave beyond the boundaries drawn by the system);

6. Professional education in different fields tends to develop awareness/unawareness to different levels of beneficence. (For example: In the United States professional training for social work tends to open awareness to the full range of beneficence more than does professional training for law);

7. Different cultures can predispose their members to emphasize one level of beneficence over the others. (For example: According to the statement of Fox/Swazey that for the Chinese "the bedrock and point of departure of medical morality lie in the quality of these human relationships: in how correct, respectful, harmonious, complementary, and reciprocal they are" ([16], 650), we would expect this culture to emphasize social beneficence more than individual beneficence. By contrast, the proclivity in U. S. culture is to make the perspective of the individual realm dominant, if not exclusive. This cultural predisposition finds expression in statements such as that by George Annas: "The core legal and ethical principle that underlies all human interactions in medicine is autonomy" ([2], 5).

8. Most issues of healthcare ethics have significance on all three levels, but more often than not an issue has a primary level of ethical significance that constitutes the ethical center of the issue. The other spheres should be resolved relative to this ethical center. For example, refusing treatment is primarily a question of individual ethics—but institutions and society need to make structural protection and facilitation of this refusal a real possibility. On the other hand, developing a reasonable national health policy is essentially an issue of societal ethics, where individuals and institutions must subordinate their specific interests to the greater good of society.

This is a beginning list of some obvious differences that exist between these realms of ethical reality. Much work remains to be done in understanding such differences across these spheres.

Professional training for social work tends to open awareness to the full range of beneficence more than does professional training for law.

III. Further Conclusions and Explorations

Having roughed out some key elements of an ethic of beneficence, I want to turn to further conclusions and explorations.

The Community of Concern

The keystone of beneficence is community. The very term beneficence emphasizes that we are always persons-in-relationships—social beings. It implies that the natural state of persons is reciprocal, responsive, and engaged. It understands self-giving as essential and self-realizing; it sees the love imperative primarily as an invitation to become, not as a constraint on being.

There is a presumption that the privileged agent of ethical discernment is the "community of concern."

The three-tiered model of beneficence symbolizes how thoroughly individuals are imbedded in layers of social reality: individuals exist within networks of mediating organizations and these in turn are woven into a matrix of society. Community is the ocean in which we swim.

In a beneficence ethic there is a presumption that the privileged agent of ethical discernment is the "community of concern." Certainly, individual ethics makes sense and existential ethical decisions are always made by individuals. But as the three-layered paradigm makes clear at a glance, most ethical terrain involves community. Beyond this, making normative ethical judgments involves the weighing of complex and subtle values and this emerges primarily from experience of these values—from a pool of experience wide and deep enough to do justice to the issue at hand. Here we are on the wrong track if professionals' views of patient experience are taken for patient experience; if men represent the experience of women; if doctors mediate nurses' views; if administrators speak for the general public. To weigh complex values, we need complex, first-hand experience, as well as adequate analysis of that experience.

The community of concern is constituted by whatever group is necessary to be in experiential touch with all the major facets of a beneficence question.

Gathering the key elements of this first-hand experience is what the "community of concern" is all about. This is a formal concept to be materially specified by the issue at hand. *The community of concern is constituted by whatever group is necessary to be in experiential touch with all the major facets of a beneficence question.* Lacking the full community of concern, we are in ethical trouble from the start. No individual or partial group, regardless of ethical fiber or training, can substitute for the full community of concern.

One of the first questions asked by an ethic of beneficence will be: do we have the right community for this issue?

From this perspective, hospitals represent a moral minefield. Hospitals are highly structured along lines that stratify, fragment, and compartmentalize. Such a structure is ethically inhibiting, viewed from the perspective of the community of concern because it keeps like-minded groups reflecting within their limited field of experience. Perhaps the ethics committee movement's greatest contribution can be to introduce a new paradigm of reflection and empowerment into the highly compartmentalized healthcare structure.

One of the first questions asked by an ethic of beneficence will be: do we have the right community for this issue? If not, what persons do we need to give us the necessary fullness of perspective?

Personal Qualities of Community Members

Beyond a fullness of perspectives on the issue at hand, the members of this community of concern also need to possess some basic personal qualities: a genuine respect for persons; openness to perspectives differing from their own; desire to learn and study; willingness to be wrong; ability to express challenging perspectives directly and honestly; ability to collaborate in a team effort. Ethical wisdom can emerge more consistently and efficiently from a community sharing a heavy dose of these qualities.

Shared Common Vision of Community Members

A key difference between a gathering of special interest advocates and a community of concern is that the latter share a deeper vision that binds them and their differing perspectives into a coherent whole. There may be strong differences on various perspectives of the issue, but stronger still are their grounding meanings and priorities. Selecting the community of concern involves finding persons who share this deeper vision or are capable of being called to it. This deeper vision demands attention and resources. It is not simply a given. Elsewhere I have explored how a superficial agreement about justice can hide a deeper level of strong disagreements [21]. A community of concern needs to nurture its shared vision, to test its consensus, to sharpen its definitions, to deepen it, to revise it. Neglect of this deeper vision erodes the community's ability to ethically discern.

A community of concern needs to nurture its shared vision, to test its consensus, to sharpen its definitions, to deepen it, to revise it.

Tools of Community Enablement

The community of concern needs to be enabled to do the discernment of beneficence. To harness the complexity of values and disvalues, deeper vision and complementary perspectives, and unity and differences we need instruments of enablement. We can think of these as cognitional tools and process tools.

Cognitional Tools.

Philosophical and theological ethics can help us understand the importance and role of definitions, distinctions, concepts, principles, and paradigms. These disciplines can provide formal understanding of these elements and material content for application. These disciplines can also sug-

*Such knowledge
is mystic,
affective
knowledge of
the heart and
imagination.*

gest methodologies for harnessing this complexity of elements and moving it progressively to closure.

But evaluative knowledge involved in beneficence is more than abstract concepts and cold analysis. Such knowledge is mystic, affective knowledge of the heart and imagination. Here our resources are not extensively developed, and considerable work needs to be done. Fortunately, there is a growing recognition of the direct importance of the arts and literature as tools of enablement for the discerning community. It is in this area that case studies and parables can give human breadth and depth to more discursive principles and definitions.

Group Process Tools.

To handle the complex group it has gathered, beneficence needs adequate group process. Adequate process will facilitate a fullness of reflection that: 1) is focused but not rigidly constricting; 2) is co-extensive with the length and breadth of the problem, not ignoring essential areas, not coming to premature closure; 3) attends to persons as well as issues; 4) insures input from all and monopoly of none; 5) allows for self-examination and interpersonal communication; 6) promotes open challenge and confrontation; 7) includes intellection, intuition, affect, and imagination. Front-end planning of meetings cannot guarantee these characteristics but it can go far in enabling them.

Need for Fresh Disciplines

In *The Good Society,* Bellah et al. remark, "We need experts and expert opinion, and experts can certainly help us to think about important issues. But democracy is not the rule of experts" ([3], 272). This is also true about beneficence—it is not the rule of experts but it certainly benefits from the help of experts in facing the dilemmas of beneficence. Philosophers, theologians, and lawyers have been some of the founding fathers/mothers of health care ethics. But now we need to expand the field of experts guiding this reflection.

*We need to
expand the field
of experts
guiding this
reflection.*

First, we need a broader band of ethical tradition than has been present up to this time. Fox and Swazey note—and I think legitimately—"It is primarily American analytic philosophy—with its emphasis on theory, methodology, and technique, and its utilitarian, Kantian, and 'contractarian' outlooks—in which most of the philosophers who have entered bioethics were trained" ([16], 666). Our paradigm of beneficence suggests that this narrower philosophical tradition is not enough. The latter is most comfortable in the realm of individual beneficence, and has a tendency to keep us confined to a "minimalist ethics" [8] rather than push us to the broader bands of beneficence. Political and social philosophy, Christian social teaching, and feminist thought will be especially important for an expanded philosophical horizon.

Our strong proclivity for individual beneficence is reinforced by the extensive presence in bioethics of those trained in U. S. law. Glendon emphasizes that legal training in our society is likely to bring with it a rights-laden ethos and rhetoric which "easily accommodates the economic, the immediate, and the personal dimension of a problem, while it regularly neglects the moral, the long-term, and the social implications" ([22], 171). The *Hastings Center Report*—probably the most influential and certainly longest-lived journal of bioethics—has a regular column, "At Law," but no corresponding consistent message from the social sciences.

As we move into the next phase of healthcare ethics, we will need the help of such fields as sociology, philosophy/ theology of society, anthropology, political science, public health, organizational development, and social psychology. The work of Fox/Swazey and Glendon, which sets our own ethical and legal assumptions into a broader social and multicultural context, point to the potential of such work for an expanded horizon of healthcare ethics. But at present such efforts sit at the margins of medical ethics, rather than giving it direction and leadership. I believe that in the next decades there will be a direct relationship between the level of vigor, creativity and fruitfulness of healthcare ethics and the degree to which these now-foreign disciplines assume roles of prominence and leadership. Healthcare ethics has benefited from the service of academic ethics and law, but as we move into the wider spheres of beneficence, the importance of these disciplines will legitimately wane as the role of other enabling disciplines waxes.

We will need the help of such fields as sociology, philosophy/ theology of society, anthropology, political science, public health, organizational development, and social psychology.

Shaping the Hospital to Beneficence

Rosemary Stevens remarks that the "American hospital has been— and is—a projection of a medical profession whose archetypes are science, daring, and entrepreneurship" ([54], 11). Organizations shaped by such archetypes do not promise to be adept at making beneficence decisions in terms we have discussed. If we were to reinvent the hospital to make it a better agent of beneficence, what steps might we take?

A first step would be to awaken the institution to the fact that beneficence/ethics is omnipresent—it permeates the life of the organization. Elsewhere I have argued that ethics is coextensive with human dignity: that wherever decisions are being made about the dignity of persons, we have ethical activity. In the conclusion to this article I stated: "Hospital Ethics Committees are just one of many Centers of Ethical Responsibility (CER's) in a modern health care institution; and they are far from the most important. This is so because any group that makes decisions that have impact on the dignity of persons are by definition centers of ethical responsibility. This means that trustees, senior management teams, etc., are essentially 'ethics committees' of great importance—and often even greater importance

Hospital Ethics Committees are just one of many Centers of Ethical Responsibility (CER's) in a modern health care institution; and they are far from the most important.

than the Hospital Ethics Committee. Since all of these CER's are essentially engaged in doing ethics, they improve their efforts by attending to key elements of institutional ethics" ([21], 286). Helping health care institutions increasingly shape their lives from the perspective of beneficence will involve: 1) helping them recognize the pervasive presence of beneficence/ethics—in planning, budgeting, managing, etc.; 2) helping them identify key ingredients for good decision-making—community of concern, need for analytic tools and appropriate process, and role of education; and 3) helping them build these elements into the fabric of institutional life.

More specifically, considering our model of three-tiered beneficence, I believe that health care institutions will be most myopic concerning their societal agency and responsibility. Reflecting on the history of U. S. hospitals, Stevens observes that without "financial incentives, hospitals have rarely tried to change the system in directions which would clearly be in the public interest." Rather we have a tug-of-war in which "federal and state agencies are trying to further public agendas. . . while hospitals are trying to deflect and/or resist them, in order to further their own organizational objectives" ([54], 353).

Hospitals need to develop a conscience concerning sphere 2b of beneficence—a moral sensitivity to their societal role and their responsibility for the healthcare common good. They need to become a more vigorous part of the community of concern shaping our health care system, and less an agent of special interest pressure. They need to invest time in understanding health issues from the perspective of community good, not merely from the viewpoint of organizational benefit. They need to take time to develop some consensus about what an adequate health system for our society would look like: what percentage of the GNP we can reasonably spend on health care—relative to the other needs of the common good. If the health care professionals of our nation do not have a coherent set of questions and answers around these central issues, we should not be surprised if politicians reduce such issues to matters of balancing a budget. However one judges the substance of the plan proposed by Physicians for a National Health Program, their substantial efforts at advocacy for the common good present us with an outstanding—and almost unique—example of "2b conscience" in the world of healthcare organizations and professionals.

In approaching these issues, the larger hospital community can benefit from some learnings of ethics committees. Two learnings are of special importance. First, education is an essential element for good ethical decision-making. Balancing and weighing complex and subtle dimensions of human, interdependent good requires an informed community. Devising an appropriate public policy on quality, access and financing of health care requires a community of committed and informed discussants. If hospitals are to move toward an ethic of societal interest, they will have to engage their governance and management in ongoing education about such issues. Good institutional ethics implies a commitment to substantive education for trustees

Hospitals need to develop a moral sensitivity to their societal role and their responsibility for the health-care common good.

If hospitals are to move toward an ethic of societal interest, they will have to engage their governance and management in ongoing education about such issues.

To what extent does a typical hospital board represent the community of concern one would want for making the range of beneficence decisions sketched above?

and management teams. Traditionally, hospitals are slow to recognize educational need and to fund educational efforts in proportion to their importance.

Beyond this lies the second and even more fundamental question of the community of concern. To what extent does a typical hospital board represent the community of concern one would want for making the range of beneficence decisions sketched above? If it is lacking, how should we enhance this community in order to give it more the character of an appropriate community of concern? For example, two perspectives that are commonly absent from governance that seem essential are—internally—the nursing perspective and—externally—the public health perspective.

Questions of selection of leadership—in terms of specific criteria that enjoy consensus among the selection group, and effective ways of using these criteria to screen candidates—has not received much ethical attention. Given the central role of the community of concern in making good ethical decisions, hospitals should give considerably more attention to the substance and process of leadership selection [19, 20].

New Phase, New Tasks for Healthcare Ethics

I believe that Phase One of healthcare ethics is coming to a close. This first phase has spanned the last 20 years and generated literature, processes, and tools that have primarily focused on individual ethics. Given our cultural fixation on individual rights and the paternalistic ethos and mores of U.S. medical care in those years, such an emphasis is historically understandable. But there are increasing signs that the limits of such emphasis are being experienced and the need for attention to the broader realms of beneficence is being recognized.

In Phase Two, an unaccustomed set of questions arise at the very start of ethical examination of an issue: what significance does this issue have on the three levels of beneficence? Which level(s) need we deal with? Which level is the decisive level of concern? Only when we have answered these questions adequately can we effectively do ethics—by gathering the appropriate community of concern and providing the level-appropriate tools of enablement to the community.

Moving from Individual to Social Perspective: Two Examples

Now I want to consider two examples that illustrate: 1) the U.S. tendency to analyze and resolve issues as if they were issues of individual ethics; 2) how differently the issues are discussed and resolved when we locate them on the institutional or societal level.

Case Consultation—An Issue of Institutional, Not Individual Ethics

First let's look at the question of case consultation as a function of ethics committees. In an article, "A Paradigm Shift for Case Consultation" [17], a colleague and I have argued in substance—though not in these terms—that the common practice of ethics committees is to treat case consultations as a series of difficult individual cases. In effect, we are treating the problem as one with its center of gravity on the level of individual ethics. Our suggestion is that we should move our gaze to the institutional level of ethical reality and define the problem as one of institutional ethics. *If we see the cases that come to the IEC as symptoms of institutional ethical malaise, we will diagnose the institution's problem and treat this institutional problem, rather than intervening on a case-by-case basis.* Our argument is developed in two theses.

If we see the cases that come to the IEC as symptoms of institutional ethical malaise, we will diagnose the institution's problem and treat this institutional problem, rather than intervening on a case-by-case basis.

Thesis One: Case consultation by an ethics committee should be recognized as an institutional embarrassment to be eliminated as soon as possible and replaced by institutional change— consistent, effective patterns of case conferencing by staff as a routine part of patient care. The chronic problem is an organizational deficit—the absence of adequate discussion of patient care by the community of key stakeholders in the case. Because the worst effects of this chronic deficit have finally come to our attention, the "ethics case consultation," a stop-gap intervention, has been invented. Using Howard Brody's metaphor of ethics-as-conversation, we would argue that because appropriate conversations were not being held by the right people, at the right times, and in the right places, the ethics case consultation was invented to assure that at least some conversations, with some of the right persons, were being held somewhere. Given this persistent institutional deficit, the "ethics case consultation" does provide some symptomatic relief, but leaves the fundamental ethical problem—on the institutional level—unresolved. So we find ourselves in the ironic but not uncommon situation in which amelioration in terms of individual ethics becomes a disservice in terms of institutional ethics.

The "ethics case consultation" does provide some symptomatic relief, but leaves the fundamental ethical problem—on the institutional level—unresolved.

We propose an approach that promises more widespread and abiding results because it addresses the problem on the level of institutional ethics. Most simply put, it involves changing institutional systems and structures, as well as staff understandings and behaviors, so that the primary care community (patient, loved ones, and the clinical professionals involved in giving care) discuss the ethical dimensions of cases effectively, consistently, and adequately in the setting of care. This means institutionalizing the consistent and effective use of case conferences at the unit level.

To achieve this, a number of elements will be needed: 1) an institution will need to develop a consensus across key groups of professionals, from trustees to technicians, that case conferencing is not a soft issue or peripheral concern, but instead is an essential element of excellence in patient care; 2) an institution will need to identify the elements of a case conference and when such a conference would be needed; 3) an institution will need systems and structures to support this practice. These include policies, procedures, integration into the quality assurance process, orientation, credentialing, etc.; 4) an institution will need to provide education so that key publics share a common fund of knowledge, including familiarity with: a) the cases that have shaped the current ethical and legal understanding of our culture; b) the boundaries set by legislative and administrative bodies, and positions taken by major religions, cultural groups, institutions, and professional societies; c) basic concepts, definitions, and principles of the current discussion (e.g., autonomy, informed consent, competence, etc.); 5) an institution will also be helped by a methodology or protocol for conferencing. This overall methodology will attend to three phases of the case conference: preparation, conduct of the conference, and follow-up.

Thesis Two: Troubling cases, beyond their central significance for individuals, are privileged opportunities for institutional self-awareness, analysis, and evolution. Therefore, the ethics committee should continue to commit some of its energies to case review. Such case review, however, is not aimed at resolving an individual case—that is the task of the unit-based case conference—but at institutional reform. For the ethics committee, the case review becomes a tool of institutional change and reform. Institutional needs are consistently revealed in the sustained conversations of an interdisciplinary group about individual cases. There are other ways to uncover such needs, but case review is a rich source of institutional insight.

While the position developed above demands further discussion, to be sure, the point here is simply that in addressing the question as one of institutional ethics rather than individual ethics, a different kind of argument takes place, different conclusions emerge, and different imperatives and behaviors are called for.

Affirmative Action—A Question of Societal, Not Individual Ethics

Daniel Maguire, in his book, *A Case for Affirmative Action* [31], argues that the discussion of affirmative action has been crippled by the U. S. fixation at the level of individual morality. Affirmative action, according to Maguire, is first and foremost a question of societal ethics (in my terms), of social and distributive justice (in his terms).

Maguire uses justice as his central moral principle (I use beneficence) and he distinguishes two, not three, levels of justice concern. He also uses a triangle, where I use three concentric circles. I see these differences not in conflict with but as complementary to the ideas developed above. Following Maguire's argument in some detail can enrich our discussion and provide a fresh view of these questions.

Maguire's foundation is the conviction that we are not merely individuals; "we are social individuals, and there are three fundamental modes

Troubling cases, beyond their central significance for individuals, are privileged opportunities for institutional self-awareness, analysis, and evolutio

In addressing the question as one of institutional ethics rather than individual ethics, a different kind of argument takes place, different conclusions emerge, and different imperatives and behaviors are called for.

of sociality to which the three kinds of justice correspond. . . .We relate on a one-to-one basis (individual justice); the individual relates to the social whole (social justice); and the representatives of the social whole relate to individuals (distributive). When, for example, we talk about fulfilling contracts or repairing injuries done to discreet individuals, we are speaking of individual justice. When we speak of modes of indebtedness to the social whole exemplified by such things as taxes, jury duty, and eminent domain, we are speaking of forms of social justice. And when we speak of distributing the goods and bads of society fairly (largely through the instrumentality of government), we are speaking of distributive justice. Though social and distributive justice are distinct forms of justice, both relate to the common good and are thus coordinates" (72-73). Elsewhere Maguire illustrates this graphically as a triangle [30].

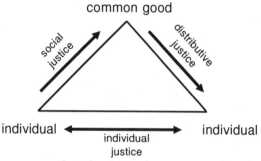

Maguire warns us that the "American context is a breeding ground for special errors in understanding justice." (75) Ours is a culture that is gravely prone to fixation at the level of individual justice. "Fixation on individual justice means that only one form of social relationship is acknowledged—the one-to-one kind. Such a fixationist could say, in fidelity to his own premises: 'If I made a deal with you, I will honor it; if I hurt you, I will make amends; but if I did neither, bug off!' If there is only individual justice, those would be the words of a just man." (76) It will come as no surprise when the U. S. mentality approaches the question of affirmative action and sees it in terms of individual justice. Maguire notes that this is precisely what the U. S. Supreme Court has done: "the Court has been demonstrating convincingly that it does not have an adequate understanding of the ethical concepts of social or distributive justice to handle the question with clarity or consistency. Affirmative action is an issue of social-distributive justice. The Court usually attempts to handle it using the concepts appropriate to individual. . . justice. It doesn't work." (vii)

The very fabric of our society is interlaced with systems and structures that disempower individuals and groups, based on race and gender.

According to Maguire, the problem we face is not primarily that individuals are acting unfairly, based on race and gender, but that the *very fabric of our society is interlaced with systems and structures that disempower individuals and groups, based on race and gender.* We need to recognize that when the social fabric is characterized by in-structured inequities and monopolies of power, distributive justice demands a restructuring and redistribution by the agents of the common good. Social justice requires that individuals contribute to and collaborate in this effort. Maguire explains:

> "Although individual good is set within the common good, the two are not identical. This raises the possibility that the two might conflict. Relative to preferential affirmative action, this leads to the critical question: *May individual rights be sacrificed to the common good?* To rephrase the question: Does it make any sense to say that individuals who have done no wrong or who have assumed no contractual obligations should, at times, be required in a just society to sacrifice their privileges, rights, possessions, or career goals for broader social aims? The answer to this question is yes. And, more disconcertingly yet, these sacrifices will not be required equally of all but only of some, and even then often somewhat happenstantially. Furthermore, any society that survives does so by living with this enigmatic fact of life—however many monuments that society may build to the individual." (104)

Does it make any sense to say that individuals who have done no wrong or who have assumed no contractual obligations should, at times, be required to sacrifice their privileges, rights, possessions, or career goals for broader social aims?

To see affirmative action as an issue of social/distributive justice means recognizing that society has an imbedded network of social systems that result in grave injustices for identifiable groups. Such groups are not just "slowed down," they are fundamentally disempowered and severely and chronically deprived of access to the common good. Therefore there is an imperative—grounded in social/distributive justice—to empower these groups through preferential social aid and thereby "end their excommunication from the common good."

Then Maguire faces the next task of societal ethics—developing the more specific criteria and principles needed for making practical decisions and applying this analysis to life. Maguire offers four criteria for enforced preferential aid and claims that these four are fulfilled paradigmatically by blacks, but that three other groups—women, American Indians, and some segments of the Hispanic population also meet these criteria. The four criteria are these:

1) No alternatives to enforced preference are available. Maguire notes that "even when the federal government has insisted on the rights of blacks through executive orders, rulings of the Supreme Court, and formal legislative action, resistance has been formidable" (143). Voluntarism has repeatedly and decisively failed. The only realistic resolution involves enforced redistribution;

Voluntarism has repeatedly and decisively failed. The only realistic resolution involves enforced redistribution.

2) The prejudice against the group must reach the level of depersonalization. Depersonalizing prejudice "tells the victims that their very humanity is deficient" (143). Among the evidence offered by Maguire to substantiate this criterion are the results of a study re-

ported in the Northwestern University Law Review showing that it is only after the third grade that black children begin to fall behind, and that this seems to relate to their discovery of their low status in society (149);

3) The bias against the group is not private or narrowly localized but is rather entrenched in the culture and distributive systems of the society. Maguire then examines the status of the black community concerning: health, unemployment, education, and housing. In this last category he notes a study which estimates "that if the population density of some of Harlem's worst blocks were extended to all of New York City, the entire population of the United States could fit into just three of New York's boroughs!" (162);

4) The members of the victim group must be visible as such and thus lack an avenue of escape from their disempowered status (165). "In slaving times it was said that the advantage of black slaves was that nature had branded them from head to toe."

Maguire's full argument demands the several hundred pages he devotes to it. My overview attempts only to show the contours of a discussion that grasps the ethics of affirmative action as a question that must be handled on the level of societal ethics, not merely on the level of individual ethics.

Other examples could illustrate this same point. Daniel Callahan has for decades been treating societal questions with the expanse and complexity they deserve. His treatment of abortion [7], healthcare reform [9], and human mortality [10] are splendid examples of the kind of creative, strenuous, and scholarly work that societal ethics demands.

Codes of Ethical Wholeness

This model of beneficence would urge us to formulate our codes of ethics to cover all the realms of ethics. One notable example of such a comprehensive professional code that could serve as a model is the National Association of Social Workers' Code of Ethics [26]. This code identifies six areas of concern: 1) personal conduct; 2) duties to clients; 3) duties to colleagues; 4) duties to employers; 5) duties to the Social Work Profession; 6) duties to society. Not only does this code recognize this comprehensive range of concerns, it also translates each area into an effective and realistic level of specificity.

Even some of the recent attempts to develop richer professional medical codes stay within the realm of individual ethics ([38], 203-206). Certainly physicians owe priority to their patients. Their codes should reflect this. But these codes should also speak at some level of specificity about duties on the organizational level—to hospitals, to nurses, to the medical

If the population density of some of Harlem's worst blocks were extended to all of New York City, the entire population of the United States could fit into just three of New York's boroughs!

Daniel Callahan has for decades been treating societal questions with the expanse and complexity they deserve.

This model of beneficence would urge us to formulate our codes of ethics to cover all the realms of ethics.

staff, as well as on the societal level—to help develop and maintain a health care system with just patterns of access and reasonable parameters of quality and cost.

The St. Joseph Health System in Orange, California has promoted the development of physician value statements among the medical staffs of its hospitals. These "ethical codes" take some meaningful steps in including the broader ranges of beneficence, as the following example from one of the System's hospitals illustrates.

A Commitment to Values

Medical Staff
Queen of the Valley Hospital
Napa, California

We are committed to being leaders in shaping our society's health care. We believe that we must serve the broad health needs of persons: spiritual, physical and emotional.

We stand at the heart of the health care services, interacting with patients, families, professional colleagues, agencies and institutions. As medical staff members of the Queen of the Valley Hospital, we are associated with an institution which has a strong tradition of values. We are vital partners in the concrete expression of those values; therefore, we offer the following statement.

WE BELIEVE:

- life is sacred. We should courageously defend life but should not do so when all attempts to preserve life are futile.

- sickness and healing are important events that affect all dimensions of a person's life. Physicians should address the spiritual, emotional and social dimensions of illness.

- informed, competent patients are their own primary decision-makers. Our decisions about patient care involve the professional expertise and the personal values of the patient, family and professionals. The conscience of physicians should be respected by patients and institutions.

- quality patient care is effected by clear, respectful communication between patient, family and health care professionals.

- nurses have a unique relationship with doctors, patients and the patients' families. Their presence and expertise is of great importance in the care of patients.

- human dignity demands that our society assure universal access to an adequate level of health care. Physicians should play an active role in this process.

- physicians should serve on medical staff and peer review committees. Physicians should constructively challenge the goals and directions of the institution and examine with insight their own role and level of performance.

- only a community of shared vision can achieve these far-reaching goals. We commit ourselves to be part of a community to work for these goals. We recognize that resources are limited and require hard choices. We will join in making such choices as fairly and accountably as possible.

We believe that we must serve the broad health needs of persons: spiritual, physical, social and emotional.

Human dignity demands that our society assure universal access to an adequate level of health care.

*To what extent
should IEC's
become agents
of social change
within their own
institutions and
within the larger
community?*

Ethics committees could revisit the issue of their own mission/purpose statement in light of these three realms of ethical complexity. Are there some areas that deserve more explicit attention? If so, would this involve a change/expansion of membership? Does this modify the traditional big three activities of the committee: consultation, education, policy review and development? To what extent should IEC's become agents of social change within their own institutions and within the larger community?

Hospitals could develop a code of ethics for their institution. Ethics committees could help by developing a draft of such a code. It would give priority to organizational good, but explicitly set this within the complexity of individual and societal good. Such an exercise would contribute to the self-education of the ethics committee and offer an opportunity to engage in the ethical education of both governance and management. Such a code of ethics could involve the medical staff and employees of the hospital in its evolution.

As a nation, we do not have a "National Code of Health Care Ethics." One modest but real contribution to the realization of an ethically sound national health program could be a broad effort to formulate such a "National Code." This would press us to engage in the troublesome but indispensable discussion of key elements of the health care common good, instead of merely debating concrete proposals without a larger frame of reference. It would also force us to struggle with the interdependencies and shifting hierarchies that prevail between these three spheres of beneficence.

Beneficence ethics invites us to evolve codes of ethics that explicitly face the conflicting loyalties that confront us within each sphere and across the spheres of the comprehensive picture of beneficence.

Global Beneficence

*There is a
fourth sphere of
beneficence
about which I
have been silent
up to now—the
sphere of global
beneficence.*

There is a fourth sphere of beneficence about which I have been silent up to now—the sphere of global beneficence. The concern here is the common good of the globe. It represents a still broader, more complex and vastly more difficult realm of values/goods/loyalties in conflict. I mention it here only to sketch the complete parameters of a beneficence ethic, not to fill in the details. However, two perspectives deserve passing mention:

1) Global beneficence considers the good of the planet itself as an ecology and environment for the human family. It demands that we think in space- and time-frames that are alien and alienating to our current patterns. Our concern here is the kind of health environment we are shaping for the global generations to come.

2) Global beneficence looks at the balanced allocation of healthcare resources throughout the global community. While allowing for differences between nations, it must explore the acceptable limits to those differences and the responsibilities of wealthy nations for the health care of poorer nations. An ethic of beneficence not only presses us to recognize this further realm but it also offers a framework—analogous to the other spheres—for filling in the specifics.

Summary

Drawing on the Christian tradition of beneficence as the heart of morality and ethics offers us the chance to view the enterprise of healthcare ethics from a fresh perspective. It highlights the constant process of resolving our conflicting values/loyalties on three levels of human reality—the individual, the organizational, and the societal. It invites us to develop a consciousness of new ethical horizons and to create the ethical tools needed by the community to meet the challenges of these new realms.

Bibliography

1. Anspach R. R. "Prognostic conflict in life-and-death decisions: the organization as an ecology of knowledge." *J. Hlth Soc. Behav.* 28, 215, 1987.
2. Annas, G. "Life, Liberty, and Death," *Health Management Quarterly*, vol. 12, no. 1, 5-8, 1990.
3. Bellah, R., Madsen, R., Sullivan, W., Swidler, A., Tipton, S. *The Good Society*, Alfred A. Knopf, New York, 1991.
4. Bellah, R., Sullivan, W. "The Professions and the Common Good: Vocation/Profession/Career," *Religion and Intellectual Life*, Spring, vol. IV, no. 3, 7-20, 1987.
5. Bouchard, C., Pollock, J. "Condoms and the Common Good," *Second Opinion*, 12, 98-106, 1989.
6. Brody, H. "Causing, Intending, and Assisting Death," *The Journal of Clinical Ethics*, vol. 4, no. 2, 112-117, 1993.
7. Callahan, D. *Abortion: Law, Choice, and Morality*, Macmillan, New York, 1970.
8. Callahan, D. "Minimalist Ethics," *Hastings Center Report*, vol. 11, no. 5: October, 19-25, 1981.
9. Callahan, D. *What Kind of Life*, Simon and Schuster, New York, 1990.
10. Callahan, D. *The Troubled Dream of Life*, Simon and Schuster, New York, 1993.
11. Carpentier, R. "Vers une morale de la charité," *Gregorianum* 34, 47-62, 1953.
12. Childress, James. "Just War Theories: The Bases, Interrelations, Priorities, and Functions of Their Criteria," *Theological Studies*, vol. 39, no. 3, 427-445, 1978.
13. Curran, C. *Toward an American Catholic Moral Theology*, Notre Dame University, Notre Dame, Indiana, 1987.
14. Dewey, J. "The Nature of Moral Theory," in R. Ekman (ed.), *Readings in the Problems of Ethics*, Charles Scribner's Sons, New York, 4-8, 1965.
15. Farrell, W. "A Note on the Abortion Debate," *America*, January 27, 52-53, 1990.

16. Fox, R., and Swazey, J. "Medical Morality is not Bioethics—Medical Ethics in China and the United States," *Essays in Medical Sociology*, Transaction Books, New Brunswick, 645-671, 1988.

17. Glaser, J., and Miller, R. "A Paradigm Shift for Ethics Committees and Case Consultation: A Modest Proposal," *HEC Forum*, 5 (2), 83-88, 1993.

18. Glaser, J, "Governing Boards as Facilities' Principal Ethics Committees," *Health Progress*, Jan/Feb., 70-73, 96, 1987.

19. Glaser, J, "Selecting the Cream of the Crop," *Health Progress*, July-August, 86-89, 1989.

20. Glaser, J, "Selecting the Cream of the Crop (Part II)," *Health Progress*, April, 14-16, 33, 1992.

21. Glaser, J. "Hospital Ethics Committees: One of Many Centers of Responsibility," *Theoretical Medicine*, 10, 275-288, 1989.

22. Glendon, M. *Rights Talk, The Free Press*, Macmillan, New York, 1991.

23. Griffin, L. "The Church, Morality, and Public Policy," in C. Curran (ed.), *Moral Theology: Challenges for the Future*, Paulist Press, New York, 334-354, 1990.

24. Gustafson, J. "Moral Discourse About Medicine: A Variety of Forms," *The Journal of Medicine and Philosophy*, 15, 125-142, 1990.

25. Hardin, G. "The Tragedy of the Commons," *Science*, 162, 1243-1248, 1968.

26. Hepworth, D., and Larsen, J. *Direct Social Work Practice: Theory and Skills*, Wadsworth, Belmont, CA., 1990.

27. Jennings, B., Callahan, D., Wolf, S., et al. "The Public Duties of the Professions," *Hastings Center Report*, vol. 17, no. 1, 1-20, 1987.

28. Jonsen, A., Siegler, M., Winslade, W. *Clinical Ethics*, Macmillan Publishing Co. New York, 1982.

29. Maguire, D. *The Moral Choice*, Winston Press, Minneapolis, 1979.

30. Maguire, D. "The Primacy of Justice in Moral Theology," *Horizons* 10: 72-85, 1983.

31. Maguire, D. *A Case for Affirmative Action*, Shepherd Inc., Dubuque, 1992.

32. McCormick, R. "Notes on Moral Theology," *Theological Studies*, vol. 39, no. 2., 76-136, 1978.

33. McCormick, R. *Doing Evil to Achieve Good*, Loyola University, Chicago, 1978.

34. McCormick, R. "Notes on Moral Theology," *Theological Studies*, vol. 42, no. 1, 74-121, 1981.

35. McCormick, R. "Bioethics in the Public Forum," *Milbank Memorial Fund Quarterly/Health and Society*, vol. 61, no. 1, 113-126, 1983.

36. Maritain, Jacques. *Man and the State*, University of Chicago Press, Chicago, 1951.

37. Murray, J. C. *We Hold These Truths*, Sheed & Ward, Kansas City, MO, 1988.

38. Pellegrino, E., and Thomasma, D. *For the Patient's Good: The Restoration of Beneficence in Health Care*, Oxford University Press, New York, 1988.

39. Pope Pius XI. "Quadragesimo Anno," in C. Carlen (ed.), *The Papal Encyclicals: 1903-1939*, Pieran Press, Raleigh, 1931.

40. Quill, T., Cassel, C. "Care of the Hopelessly Ill: Proposed Clinical Criteria for Physician-Assisted Suicide," *New England Journal of Medicine*, vol. 327, no. 19, 1380-1384, 1992.

41. Rahner, K. "Über die Einheit von Nächsten- und Gottesliebe," *Schriften Zur Theologie, VI*, Benziger Verlag, Einsiedeln, 277-300, 1965.

42. Rahner, K. *The Love of Jesus and the Love of Neighbor*, Crossroads, New York, 1983.

43. Schreiner, J. *Die Zehn Gebote im Leben des Gottesvolkes*, Patmos, Düsseldorf, 1966.

44. Schüller, B. "Zur theologischen Diskussion über die lex naturalis," *Theologie und Philosophie*, 4, 481-503, 1966.

45. Schüller, B. "Typen ethischer Argumentation in der katholischen Moraltheologie', Theologie und Philosophie 4, 526-550, 1970.

46. Schüller, B. "Zur Problematik allgemein verbindlicher ethischer Grundsätze," *Theologie und Philosophie*, 1, 1-23, 1970.

47. Schüller, B. "Zur Rede von der Radikalen Sittlichen Forderung," *Theologie und Philosophie*, 3, 321-341, 1971.

48. Schüller, B. "Direkte Tötung—indirekte Tötung," *Theologie und Philosophie*, 3, 341-357, 1972.

49. Schüller, B. "Neuere Beiträge zum Thema Begründung sittlicher Normen," *Theologische Berichte*, 4, 109-181, 1974.

50. Schüller, B. "Typen der Begründung Sittlicher Normen," *Concilium*, 648-654, 1976.

51. Schüller, B. "Die Bedeutung der Erfahrung für die Rechtfertigung sittlicher Verhaltensregeln," *Christlich glauben und handeln: Fragen einer fundamentalen Moraltheologie in der Diskussion*, Patmos, Düsseldorf, 261-286, 1977.

52. Schüller, B. *Die Begründung Sittlicher Urteile*, Patmos Verlag, Düsseldorf, second edition, 1980.

53. Stark, W. *The Sociology of Knowledge*, London, 1958.

54. Stevens, R. *In Sickness and in Wealth, American Hospitals in the Twentieth Century*, Basic Books, New York, 1989.

55. United States Catholic Conference Administrative Board, "Political Responsibility: Choices for the 80's," *Origins*, 13, April 12, 732-736, 1984.

56. United States Catholic Conference, *Economic Justice for All*, Washington, D.C., 1986.

57. Veatch, R. *Case Studies in Medical Ethics*, Harvard, Cambridge, 1977.

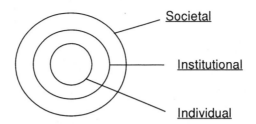

Societal

Institutional

Individual

Part II
Case Studies

Introduction

The following cases were selected with one chief purpose in mind: to give the reader and her/his community a chance to exercise thinking about ethical issues in terms of the three concentric circles—individual, institutional, societal.

These cases resemble pattern practices in a language book. After a point of grammar has been explained in the target language, such practices give the reader a chance to "overlearn" the point that has just been explained. By repeating the pattern over and over, one meets new situations spontaneously with the newly acquired way of seeing and hearing reality. The cases should have this same effect. By viewing ethical cases in terms of these three concentric circles of complexity, one can come spontaneously to perceive, explore, and resolve ethical problems in this way. This is the primary intent of the following section.

The content of the cases makes no attempt to capture the key issues facing us today. The actual cases have more to do with what stories were in the *New York Times* and *American Medical News* while I was writing this book than with anything else. These were stories that caught my attention and that invited me to turn them into case studies. This means that more important case material is missing than is included in the following pages. But since I hope that this book will occasion a living dialogue between reader and the events of now, I am not concerned about all the important issues that do not appear here.

I chose to develop five questions for each of the three areas—individual, institutional, societal—because that made up a reasonable one-page reflection/education tool. There is nothing more to it than that. This actually leads to masking the fact that for each issue there is a central dimension of importance and two subordinate dimensions. But one of the lessons of beneficence is that what we can accomplish in any given time and space is severely limited. Seen in this way, the following cases represent another example of creaturely freedom.

Hopefully, those who use this book will do many more things with these cases than I could ever imagine (I hope that you will let me know what creative uses you have made of these modest offerings). But just to suggest some directions of further uses, think about the following:

- ask for each case: what—if any—is the central dimension of ethical importance for this case; what secondary, what tertiary dimension?

- what are 3-5 more issues on each level that need to be addressed?

- what *ethical principles* are central for each dimension of ethical reality in this case?

- how would you *define* the ethical reality on the different levels of ethical significance? (see example after case #50)

- ask each person in your group to find a case and develop issues on each of three levels for discussion/resolution.

- develop questions that explore the fourth dimension of global issues.

My primary hope is that the following cases will help you to build a community of trust, of open and challenging communication, of hope—a community bent on beneficence. Without that, all of our ethical utterances are "sounding brass and tinkling cymbals".

Case Studies

#1: REPORTING ADDITIONAL INCOME

Mary McCarthy has five children, ranging in age from six months to eight years. Mary is a single mother and she supports her family with her AFDC check. Occasionally Mary needs additional income to meet unexpected expenses. In such cases she can babysit for various neighbors. She knows that she is required by law to report this additional income to the welfare department, but she has never done so because she cannot live on the reduced payments that would result from such disclosure. Mary's social work therapist becomes aware of this situation, but Mary says frankly: "If you show me how I can make ends meet on my AFDC checks alone, I'll be glad to follow your advice."

INDIVIDUAL ISSUES	strongly agree	agree	not sure	disagree	strongly disagree
1. The social worker has an ethical obligation to report fraudulent behavior to her agency and to local authorities.	❑	❑	❑	❑	❑
2. The only obligation to the client is to make her aware of the consequences of her behavior.	❑	❑	❑	❑	❑
3. The social worker should not let her professional judgment be clouded by her client's financial problems.	❑	❑	❑	❑	❑
4. The case notes should not contain any reference to this illegal activity.	❑	❑	❑	❑	❑
5. The social worker could agree with the client not to report this illegal activity so long as it never happens again.	❑	❑	❑	❑	❑

INSTITUTIONAL ISSUES					
1. The agency policy should protect the social worker from any obligation to report a client's illegal activity.	❑	❑	❑	❑	❑
2. The agency should have an emergency relief fund for workers to provide help to clients with young children who are poor.	❑	❑	❑	❑	❑
3. The agency should come down hard on welfare cheats and report all known violations by its clients.	❑	❑	❑	❑	❑

	strongly agree	agree	not sure	disagree	strongly disagree
4. Social work agencies should have strong advocacy policies and should work towards increasing welfare payments for mothers with young children.	❏	❏	❏	❏	❏
5. Agency policy should require that clients who violate the terms of AFDC be referred out to the workfare program.	❏	❏	❏	❏	❏

SOCIETAL ISSUES

	strongly agree	agree	not sure	disagree	strongly disagree
1. The welfare system is a grave injustice and should be changed by our government.	❏	❏	❏	❏	❏
2. Because the present system denies children the basic necessities, mothers who supplement their income are justified in their civil disobedience.	❏	❏	❏	❏	❏
3. We should change federal laws so that all lobbying done to improve the condition of poor children is tax-exempt.	❏	❏	❏	❏	❏
4. Resources should be taken from high tech health care and allocated to the basic needs of poor children.	❏	❏	❏	❏	❏
5. Instituting a national workfare program should be a high priority in this next legislative session.	❏	❏	❏	❏	❏

#2: CHILDREN WITHOUT WINTER CLOTHING

Three children in a family receiving public aid arrive at school inadequately dressed for the severely cold weather. The school has a policy that when this occurs, the children will be sent home in order not to encourage such parental behavior. The children are sent home. You are the social worker assigned to cases in the school. The goal of your program is the prevention of child abuse and neglect and the strengthening of families. You know that the mother has no money available to purchase adequate clothing because she has used every last cent she has to pay off more pressing bills. Neither your agency nor the school provide emergency funds for such purposes.

INDIVIDUAL ISSUES	strongly agree	agree	not sure	disagree	strongly disagree
1. The teacher should have found out more about the home situation before sending the children home.	❑	❑	❑	❑	❑
2. The mother should have budgeted her money to provide adequate clothing.	❑	❑	❑	❑	❑
3. The social worker should work to get the school to change its policy.	❑	❑	❑	❑	❑
4. The social worker should try to get clothes from friends and family.	❑	❑	❑	❑	❑
5. The social worker should help the mother develop better priorities.	❑	❑	❑	❑	❑

INSTITUTIONAL ISSUES					
1. The school should change its policy.	❑	❑	❑	❑	❑
2. The school should have a way of providing clothes for such situations.	❑	❑	❑	❑	❑
3. The social service agency should work more closely with the school to provide for such situations.	❑	❑	❑	❑	❑
4. Churches should be more involved in providing resources to schools and social agencies.	❑	❑	❑	❑	❑
5. The press and TV should help the public understand the roots of such problems.	❑	❑	❑	❑	❑

SOCIETAL ISSUES	strongly agree	agree	not sure	disagree	strongly disagree
1. The U. S. should be able to provide adequate clothing for all of its citizens.	❑	❑	❑	❑	❑
2. Resources should be provided to help this mother break out of her cycle of poverty.	❑	❑	❑	❑	❑
3. If the U. S. spent less money on unnecessary health care, we would have more resources for social needs.	❑	❑	❑	❑	❑
4. Welfare reform could eventually eliminate such problems.	❑	❑	❑	❑	❑
5. Problems such as these are most effectively resolved by appropriate public policy.	❑	❑	❑	❑	❑

#3: IS MOB MONEY ACCEPTABLE?

Long Island Jewish Medical Center in New Hyde Park, N.Y. may be forced to wrestle with its acceptance of a donation from sources under investigation for links to organized crime. It recently dedicated a $2 million bone-marrow transplant unit for children with leukemia, other blood disorders and tumors. The four-bed, 4,000 square-foot addition to the hospital is needed in a four-county area where only one other such unit exists to serve a population of more than 6 million. The name of the new entity is: The Gambino Medical and Science Foundation Bone Marrow Transplant Unit. The name honors Thomas and Joseph Gambino, sons of the late mob boss Carlo Gambino. The sons have been cited by Justice Department officials as members of a powerful crime family and indicted on criminal charges, including extortion and, in the case of Thomas Gambino, murder. For decades the Gambinos have been major donors and fundraisers for a foundation that has raised more than $12 million for the medical center. A spokesperson for the hospital stated: "We are in the business of saving lives, not substituting ourselves for appropriate judicial process."

INDIVIDUAL ISSUES	strongly agree	agree	not sure	disagree	strongly disagree
1. Taking goods that I suspect have been gotten illegally is ethically wrong.	❏	❏	❏	❏	❏
2. I should assume the best about another person until this is clearly disproved.	❏	❏	❏	❏	❏
3. When in doubt, avoid complicity with evil.	❏	❏	❏	❏	❏
4. To accept such money implies that "the end justifies the means." Such a principle is widely rejected on ethical grounds.	❏	❏	❏	❏	❏
5. If the end doesn't justify the means, nothing does.	❏	❏	❏	❏	❏

INSTITUTIONAL ISSUES					
1. The hospital spokesperson is right. Hospitals heal, courts make judgments.	❏	❏	❏	❏	❏
2. The Gambinos are innocent until proven guilty. The hospital should accept their donations until they are convicted.	❏	❏	❏	❏	❏

	strongly agree	agree	not sure	disagree	strongly disagree
3. Accepting this money sends a very bad message to patients, staff, and community: "It's the money that counts!" The hospital should decline the offer.	❏	❏	❏	❏	❏
4. The hospital should accept the money but be discreet about the source of the funds.	❏	❏	❏	❏	❏
5. This is no worse than accepting money from the federal government which subsidizes the tobacco industry—a cause of more deaths than the Gambinos.	❏	❏	❏	❏	❏

SOCIETAL ISSUES

	strongly agree	agree	not sure	disagree	strongly disagree
1. Society is challenging the tax-free status of hospitals. Such incidents foster this attitude.	❏	❏	❏	❏	❏
2. Public trust in health care professionals has eroded dramatically. A hospital's aligning with the Gambino family is a good reason for mistrust of hospitals.	❏	❏	❏	❏	❏
3. By openly accepting these funds, we can champion one of our society's richest heritages you are innocent until proven guilty.	❏	❏	❏	❏	❏
4. Politics is the art of compromise in a democracy. In the public arena, good deeds are always entangled with evil. So, take the money.	❏	❏	❏	❏	❏
5. In a society, it is essential to divide its vital functions and to respect these divisions. Courts are the societal mechanisms for determining guilt and culpability. Society suffers when hospitals make judgments appropriate for the courts.	❏	❏	❏	❏	❏

#4: PARENTS/SCHOOLS AND SAFE SEX

As of September 1992, District of Columbia high school students will be able to receive free condoms in their schools for the first time. "AIDS threatens our future, and we must teach our children how to protect themselves," said D.C. health commissioner Mohammed N. Akhter. "As a community of mothers and fathers, guardians and grandparents, we must reach out and talk to our youth. We must teach them about the risks of sexual activity so they will protect their health and their lives." Under the AIDS prevention program, students initially will attend forum sessions where sexually-transmitted diseases will be discussed. From there, students who say they are already sexually active can attend small group sessions or receive individual counseling before receiving condoms. Parents who do not want their children to receive condoms should send a letter to the principal of the school stating their objections. If the student is under 18, officials will accept the parents' wishes.

INDIVIDUAL ISSUES	strongly agree	agree	not sure	disagree	strongly disagree
1. Sexual ethics is a matter in which a high school student should be able to make her/his own decisions.	❑	❑	❑	❑	❑
2. In the area of sexuality, there are some ethical norms that individuals should conform to, and limits should be set.	❑	❑	❑	❑	❑
3. There should be a presumption that high school students are children and that their parents have a right to be involved in issues of major family importance, such as sexual behavior.	❑	❑	❑	❑	❑
4. One should wait until marriage to become sexually intimate.	❑	❑	❑	❑	❑
5. A parent who educates his/her child appropriately about sexuality has done 90% of what needs to be done to assure the child's responsible sexual behavior.	❑	❑	❑	❑	❑

	strongly agree	agree	not sure	disagree	strongly disagree

INSTITUTIONAL ISSUES

1. Schools should exercise initiative in promoting public health, and this is a good example of where they can play that role.

2. Schools should promote public health by enabling parents to better fulfill their duties, not by dealing directly with the children on such issues.

3. Schools are justified in taking decisive action for the public good when large numbers of parents have failed to do their part.

4. Schools should stick with traditional areas of learning—such as language, math, science—and keep out of delicate areas of personal values.

5. Schools are poor institutions to deal with sexual mores because they will necessarily treat the issue as one of damage control, rather than as an issue of deep personal meaning and value.

SOCIETAL ISSUES

1. By distributing condoms at school, our society is condoning adolescent promiscuity.

2. We should distribute condoms under these circumstances to prevent fatal consequences.

3. Our society should develop a comprehensive program concerning sexuality for our teenagers.

4. Our society should not let AIDS be the basis for our public policy on the broader questions of sexual behavior.

5. Our society should spend more resources on solid sexual education for our children.

#5: BANK LOANS FOR MINORITIES

Some banks make a special effort to serve the needs of poor communities. The Bank of Pleasantview hired an African-American social worker, Ms. Washington, as a liaison with the local community. She was successful in helping a number of individuals qualify for business loans, home improvement loans, and mortgages. Recently the bank revised its policy and severely reduced the funds available for such loans. In the future, Ms. Washington was to be much more "selective" in screening candidates for loans and mortgages. The bank official informed the social worker of this decision, but assured her that there was still much work she could continue to do for the local community.

INDIVIDUAL ISSUES	strongly agree	agree	not sure	disagree	strongly disagree
1. Ms. Washington should resign in protest.	❑	❑	❑	❑	❑
2. Ms. Washington should persuade the bank officers to change the new policy.	❑	❑	❑	❑	❑
3. Ms. Washington should leak this news to the media.	❑	❑	❑	❑	❑
4. Ms. Washington should throw herself into all the other ways she has been able to serve the local community and forget about the loans.	❑	❑	❑	❑	❑
5. Ms. Washington should organize minority leaders to bring pressure on the bank to change its policy.	❑	❑	❑	❑	❑

INSTITUTIONAL ISSUES					
1. The bank has no right to institute its new policy.	❑	❑	❑	❑	❑
2. The bank has no obligation to sacrifice its interests for the sake of local residents.	❑	❑	❑	❑	❑
3. Community social workers should try to influence banks in the community to better serve the needs of the poor better.	❑	❑	❑	❑	❑
4. The Board of Directors of the bank should be educated on the negative impact their restrictive policies have on the local community.	❑	❑	❑	❑	❑

	strongly agree	agree	not sure	disagree	strongly disagree

5. The local agencies (housing, development, etc.) should pressure the bank to change its policies. ❏ ❏ ❏ ❏ ❏

SOCIETAL ISSUES

1. Federal banking regulations should mandate equity in providing loans to all income levels. ❏ ❏ ❏ ❏ ❏

2. Discrimination against low-income investors should be prosecuted. ❏ ❏ ❏ ❏ ❏

3. Our government should provide tax incentives to promote loans to low-income clients. ❏ ❏ ❏ ❏ ❏

4. There should be banking standards that insist on setting aside money for poor clients. ❏ ❏ ❏ ❏ ❏

5. Government interference in these matters should be avoided. ❏ ❏ ❏ ❏ ❏

#6: TWILIGHT OF THE GOLDS

In a 1993 play, "The Twilight of the Golds," by Jonathan Tolins, Rob and Suzanne Stein debate whether Suzanne should have an abortion after being told by a doctor that the male fetus she is carrying has a gene that probably will lead to homosexuality. The wife's gay brother, David, tries to talk her out of it, discovering in the process that his semi-estranged mother and father (Phyllis and Walter Gold) might have terminated him had they been provided with similar information. The play is not based on actual diagnostic capability or current genetic science, but the direction of development in both areas indicates that we may soon be faced with just such choice in the not-too-distant future. Given the development in genetic engineering, it seems within the realm of possibility that we may some day be able not only to detect homosexuality in utero, but also to intervene genetically and change the fetus' sexual orientation.

INDIVIDUAL ISSUES	strongly agree	agree	not sure	disagree	strongly disagree
1. Homosexuality should be seen as genetic error and corrected if possible.	❑	❑	❑	❑	❑
2. Homosexuality is primarily a question of lifestyle and free choice.	❑	❑	❑	❑	❑
3. Homosexuality is a given of nature, just like heterosexuality.	❑	❑	❑	❑	❑
4. Homosexual orientation is neutral, but homosexual activity is wrong.	❑	❑	❑	❑	❑
5. It will be advisable to change a homosexual fetus' sexual orientation through genetic intervention when that is possible.	❑	❑	❑	❑	❑

INSTITUTIONAL ISSUES

	strongly agree	agree	not sure	disagree	strongly disagree
1. The American Psychiatric Association for years now has ceased considering homosexuality as a mental illness. It's about time!	❑	❑	❑	❑	❑
2. Schools should help children overcome the homophobia of our culture.	❑	❑	❑	❑	❑
3. The Catholic Church should stand firm in its position that homosexuality as an orientation is not immoral, but homosexual activity is immoral.	❑	❑	❑	❑	❑

	strongly agree	agree	not sure	disagree	strongly disagree

4. The media should do more to clarify the difference between homophobia and legitimate negative judgments about homosexuality. ❑ ❑ ❑ ❑ ❑

5. Health professionals should work to slow down genetic progress so that our ethical categories come closer to matching our capacity to manipulate life. ❑ ❑ ❑ ❑ ❑

SOCIETAL ISSUES

1. The military policy of "Don't ask, don't tell" is clearly unfair to homosexuals. ❑ ❑ ❑ ❑ ❑

2. We should develop national guidelines concerning prenatal diagnosis of homosexuality before the possibility is upon us. ❑ ❑ ❑ ❑ ❑

3. Society would lose great human resources if we deliberately reduced the number of homosexual persons being born. ❑ ❑ ❑ ❑ ❑

4. More public resources should be dedicated to clarifying homosexuality in our culture. ❑ ❑ ❑ ❑ ❑

5. The Human Genome Project invests only a fraction of its funds in social/legal/ethical research. This creates a serious imbalance between technical can-do and ethical know-how. ❑ ❑ ❑ ❑ ❑

#7: VOLUNTARY HEALTH RISKS—WHO PAYS?

Alcohol abuse cost the U.S. health care system $85.8 billion in 1988. The cost of cigarette smoking totals over $65 billion annually. Costs related to obesity now surpass $27 billion per year. As the United States moves to reduce the staggering explosion in health care costs, the American Medical Association recently revealed that at least 25 cents of every health care dollar is spent on the treatment of diseases or disabilities that result from potentially changeable behaviors. In 1993 the number of estimated deaths as a result of smoking-related illnesses was at 419,000. This represents 20% of all annual deaths. According to Louis Sullivan, former Secretary of Health and Human Services, every person in the U. S. pays $221 annually for the health expenses of smokers alone. This comes out of the pockets of smokers and nonsmokers alike.

INDIVIDUAL ISSUES	strongly agree	agree	not sure	disagree	strongly disagree
1. Smoking is ethically wrong: there can be no justification.	❑	❑	❑	❑	❑
2. Smoking is as much caused by cultural, socioeconomic factors as by individual choice.	❑	❑	❑	❑	❑
3. Smokers and fat-eaters are victims of corporate America.	❑	❑	❑	❑	❑
4. Alcoholism is a disease more than it is a free choice.	❑	❑	❑	❑	❑
5. Smoking, eating habits and alcohol consumption are issues of lifestyle more than they are issues of ethics.	❑	❑	❑	❑	❑

INSTITUTIONAL ISSUES

	strongly agree	agree	not sure	disagree	strongly disagree
1. McDonald's has a duty to help change America's eating habits in a healthier direction.	❑	❑	❑	❑	❑
2. Insurance companies should set premiums based on lifestyle choices.	❑	❑	❑	❑	❑
3. Schools should provide in-depth courses on issues of healthy lifestyle.	❑	❑	❑	❑	❑
4. Hospital cafeterias should provide only healthy foods.	❑	❑	❑	❑	❑

	strongly agree	agree	not sure	disagree	strongly disagree
5. TV is a major factor in promoting the unhealth of America. This industry should change its behavior.	❏	❏	❏	❏	❏

SOCIETAL ISSUES

	strongly agree	agree	not sure	disagree	strongly disagree
1. Just as we charge an alcohol tax, we should tax food according to its saturated fat content.	❏	❏	❏	❏	❏
2. We should increase the alcohol tax and use this for education and prevention concerning alcohol.	❏	❏	❏	❏	❏
3. All government subsidies for tobacco should stop immediately.	❏	❏	❏	❏	❏
4. Advertising for products that cause health problems should be prohibited—for example: cigarettes, fatty foods, beer.	❏	❏	❏	❏	❏
5. U. S. health care allocates less than 5% for prevention; this should be increased at least threefold.	❏	❏	❏	❏	❏

#8: BURN CASE—FUTILE TREATMENT?

Two sisters, in their 80s, were brought to the burn unit after an accident in which their car collided with a gasoline truck. Their burns, measured in terms of thickness and extent, were devastating. Based on the most recent statistics, there was not the remotest hope of their survival. Despite such fatal prognosis, persons in this condition often experience a window of alertness, clarity and pain-free consciousness. They often find it hard to believe that their situation is so extreme, given how they feel. But this clarity of consciousness will not last very long, and so the clinicians have a relatively small window of opportunity to discuss treatment options with such patients.

INDIVIDUAL ISSUES	strongly agree	agree	not sure	disagree	strongly disagree
1. The doctor should tell them that their condition is fatal, but that they will be kept comfortable.	❏	❏	❏	❏	❏
2. The doctor should provide all possible treatment, knowing that there could be some chance of survival.	❏	❏	❏	❏	❏
3. The doctor should provide the patients with necessary information and let them decide.	❏	❏	❏	❏	❏
4. The doctor should refuse to treat them aggressively—even if they want it—since such treatment would be useless, wasteful, an indignity.	❏	❏	❏	❏	❏
5. Doctors should use persuasion in such situations if patients fail to see the realistic picture.	❏	❏	❏	❏	❏

INSTITUTIONAL ISSUES

	strongly agree	agree	not sure	disagree	strongly disagree
1. Burn units should have guidelines discouraging aggressive treatment in such situations.	❏	❏	❏	❏	❏
2. Hospital departments should not decide who gets treated—that's for patients to decide.	❏	❏	❏	❏	❏
3. Insurance companies would act justly in refusing to pay for treatment when statistics clearly indicate that it would be futile.	❏	❏	❏	❏	❏

	strongly agree	agree	not sure	disagree	strongly disagree

4. Churches should show how religious belief relates to such practical questions. ❑ ❑ ❑ ❑ ❑

5. The media should help us all face the limits of medicine in such cases, and not fuel an unrealistic hope for medical miracles. ❑ ❑ ❑ ❑ ❑

SOCIETAL ISSUES

1. A wealthy nation such as ours should not cut corners in cases like this, where life itself is at stake. ❑ ❑ ❑ ❑ ❑

2. As a nation we would be better off if we accepted death more readily in such situations. ❑ ❑ ❑ ❑ ❑

3. We would better spend our health resources on long-term care than on such futile rescue attempts. ❑ ❑ ❑ ❑ ❑

4. As a society we should develop community norms concerning futile treatment for just such cases as these. ❑ ❑ ❑ ❑ ❑

5. Unless we urge clinicians to "push the envelope" we will not make the kind of progress that has characterized U. S. medicine. ❑ ❑ ❑ ❑ ❑

#9: HANDICAPPED CHILD—FUTILE TREATMENT?

Portia Davis sits strapped in a wheelchair at the Hospital for Sick Children in Washington, a feeding tube passing through her nose. Her tiny, pointed head jerks mildly as she passes from seizure to seizure. These small convulsions continue with barely a break in between. She has been in this condition for about two years. She has virtually no brain. Her eyes are open and she experiences sleep-wake cycles, but she is completely unresponsive and unaware of her surroundings. Her prognosis, according to all her physicians is grim—no improvement.

Portia's mother had gone for a sonogram at the 27th week of her pregnancy. It showed a severe malformation, an encephalocele—a sack protruding from the back of the fetus's head that was bigger than the head itself. Most of the brain was in the sack, where it cannot function. Mrs. Davis was told by the radiologist that Portia would be "severely brain damaged, beyond retarded." The parents asked that the pregnancy be terminated, and the physician began an intravenous drug to induce labor. But within an hour he discontinued the drug because others had warned him that the child might be born alive. The pregnancy continued to term, and the child was born alive and is now expected to survive for another five years. The hospital wants the parents to take the child home, but they refuse since they will receive no funds to care for the child. Medicaid has already expended over $500,000 on Portia's care.

INDIVIDUAL ISSUES	strongly agree	agree	not sure	disagree	strongly disagree
1. The physician should have induced labor.	❑	❑	❑	❑	❑
2. If born alive, the child should have received no life support.	❑	❑	❑	❑	❑
3. The feeding tube should be removed and Portia should be allowed to die.	❑	❑	❑	❑	❑
4. The physician should have consulted the ethics committee of the hospital about this case.	❑	❑	❑	❑	❑
5. Portia's parents should sue the physician and the hospital.	❑	❑	❑	❑	❑

INSTITUTIONAL ISSUES

	strongly agree	agree	not sure	disagree	strongly disagree
1. In such cases the hospital policy should insist on review by a multidisciplinary group (such as an ethics committee).	❑	❑	❑	❑	❑
2. The hospital should have a policy that deals with such futile care.	❑	❑	❑	❑	❑
3. The hospital seems to have played a role that is appropriate in this case.	❑	❑	❑	❑	❑
4. The hospital should refuse to provide aggressive treatment for patients in a persistent vegetative state.	❑	❑	❑	❑	❑
5. Such cases should be guided by institutional policy and not left up to the individual practice of physicians.	❑	❑	❑	❑	❑

SOCIETAL ISSUES

	strongly agree	agree	not sure	disagree	strongly disagree
1. As a nation we must protect our most vulnerable patients, such as Portia.	❑	❑	❑	❑	❑
2. It is unfair that our nation spends great sums of money on Portia but does not provide universal immunization for our children.	❑	❑	❑	❑	❑
3. When we develop a national health program, it should not pay for such care.	❑	❑	❑	❑	❑
4. Portia's condition is equivalent to brain death, and our public policy should recognize it as such.	❑	❑	❑	❑	❑
5. We should allocate a greater proportion of our health dollars for chronic care and a smaller proportion for high-tech/high-cost care.	❑	❑	❑	❑	❑

#10: HYPOPLASTIC LEFT-HEART

August 29, 1992 Catherine Grotto was born at 3 AM in New Jersey. She was full term, weighed 8 pounds, but as soon as her umbilical cord was cut, she turned blue. Doctors diagnosed hypoplastic left-heart syndrome, one of the most serious heart defects in infants. Her aorta was one-tenth the normal size, meaning oxygenated blood could not get to her body. Her heart had no left ventricle. Until a decade ago, these otherwise robust-looking infants died within days. But now a few hospitals will operate. The procedure is complex, expensive, and high-risk. About 75% of the babies do not survive. For this reason many hospitals avoid the operation—it pushes up their mortality rates. The procedure involves rerouting the heart's flow of blood, sewing the pulmonary artery to the aorta and getting the right ventricle to do the left's work. Dr. Joseph Amato performed the surgery. He stopped doing these procedures for a while because of the high death rate. But he began again because of the ones who live. The ICU care, before and after surgery, and the surgery have nearly exhausted the family's $500,000 lifetime cap for a dependent. And two more operations will be needed to complete the repair. The parents fear that they might lose their home, and the child's mother is concerned that her other children will suffer—she has three others, and the oldest is six. "If I'm doing something with them and Catherine's monitor starts buzzing, I have to drop everything—sometimes a couple of times an hour. The others get annoyed." But she has no second thoughts. "We chose to have her; we have to do everything we can for her."

INDIVIDUAL ISSUES	strongly agree	agree	not sure	disagree	strongly disagree
1. The parents did the right thing in having the surgery.	❑	❑	❑	❑	❑
2. I would have done just what these parents did.	❑	❑	❑	❑	❑
3. Dr. Amato should have continued his moratorium on these surgeries.	❑	❑	❑	❑	❑
4. A physician should encourage parents to try a procedure that has a 25% success rate.	❑	❑	❑	❑	❑
5. You cannot consider money when a child's life is at stake.	❑	❑	❑	❑	❑

INSTITUTIONAL ISSUES	strongly agree	agree	not sure	disagree	strongly disagree
1. A hospital should safeguard its mortality rates by refusing to provide this procedure.	❑	❑	❑	❑	❑
2. Insurance would not be unfair if it refused to cover this procedure.	❑	❑	❑	❑	❑
3. Hospitals offering this procedure should carefully track their stats and provide this information to parents to help them decide.	❑	❑	❑	❑	❑
4. Surgeons who do this surgery bring self-interest to the decision-making process, and should have more objective colleagues help them inform the parents.	❑	❑	❑	❑	❑
5. Clergy should emphasize that there is no duty to provide this life-saving treatment for a child.	❑	❑	❑	❑	❑

SOCIETAL ISSUES

	strongly agree	agree	not sure	disagree	strongly disagree
1. Society should not allow parents to forgo such treatment.	❑	❑	❑	❑	❑
2. Child abuse laws should protect children with hypoplastic left-heart.	❑	❑	❑	❑	❑
3. A national health program should cover such procedures.	❑	❑	❑	❑	❑
4. If the U. S. were to prioritize treatments, like the state of Oregon has done, such a surgery should be far down on our list of priorities.	❑	❑	❑	❑	❑
5. We could save far more children's lives if we invested the resources used for such futile care in universal prenatal care.	❑	❑	❑	❑	❑

#11: DOCTORS REFUSE SMOKER'S BYPASS

After Harry Elphick's first heart attack last winter, doctors told him he would need a coronary bypass. But they also told him they would not even consider the heart surgery until he gave up his 25-a-day cigarette habit. Mr. Elphick, 47, did manage to quit smoking, but he never made it back to the hospital. He suffered a second heart attack and died August 13, the day he was scheduled to return for a surgical evaluation and tests. This has caused a fierce debate to rage across Britain: should doctors and hospitals be able to deny or postpone treatment to a smoker or any other patient whose behavior they regard as self-destructive? A cardiologist at the hospital clarified that this was not a moral view, simply a pragmatic stance.

It is in the clear interests of patients to give up smoking before surgery. Statistically, people who continue to smoke are poor risks for heart surgery, and even when they survive the operation, they don't live much longer than those who haven't had the surgery. Most of the public seem quite critical of the physicians' decisions and agree with a newspaper editorial that said: "A doctor's job is to heal, not judge." Physicians also pointed out that with limited money and bed space, there was nothing wrong with doctors "discriminating against those with the least chances of survival in favor of those with the best." The British Medical Association and the British Cardiac Society disapproved of systematic denial of treatment to smokers, but supported the right of doctors to use their clinical judgment in deciding whether to postpone procedures, or advise patients to reduce risky behavior like smoking. But some doctors pointed out that some surveys suggest that survival rate for nonsmokers was only slightly higher than it was for smokers.

INDIVIDUAL ISSUES	strongly agree	agree	not sure	disagree	strongly disagree
1. Individuals are responsible for their own health status.	❑	❑	❑	❑	❑
2. A patient who is a heavy smoker has no right to expect costly treatment for disease that is brought on by smoking.	❑	❑	❑	❑	❑
3. A physician's job is to heal, not to judge.	❑	❑	❑	❑	❑
4. A patient's job is to live with healthy habits, not suicidal ones.	❑	❑	❑	❑	❑
5. A physician should follow her clinical judgment about which patients can best benefit from scarce medical resources.	❑	❑	❑	❑	❑

INSTITUTIONAL ISSUES	strongly agree	agree	not sure	disagree	strongly disagree
1. Medical societies should declare prolonged smoking-cessation as a prerequisite for the treatments of diseases related to the consequences of smoking.	❑	❑	❑	❑	❑
2. Hospitals should invest more in smoking cessation programs.	❑	❑	❑	❑	❑
3. The media should hammer away at the severe health consequences of smoking.	❑	❑	❑	❑	❑
4. All health facilities should prohibit smoking anywhere on its property.	❑	❑	❑	❑	❑
5. Schools don't do nearly enough to discourage students from smoking.	❑	❑	❑	❑	❑

SOCIETAL ISSUES

	strongly agree	agree	not sure	disagree	strongly disagree
1. A national health program should have strong incentives against smoking.	❑	❑	❑	❑	❑
2. Because smoking is strongly related to socio-economic status, punitive structures will once more punish the poor.	❑	❑	❑	❑	❑
3. If tobacco tax supports health care, this may deter us from reducing smoking as aggressively as we should.	❑	❑	❑	❑	❑
4. Public policy concerning smoking can easily be based on presumptions and prejudices.	❑	❑	❑	❑	❑
5. Tobacco taxes should be dedicated only to programs that help reduce smoking by education and addiction treatment.	❑	❑	❑	❑	❑

#12: GROWTH HORMONE EXPERIMENTATION

The National Institute of Health has resumed recruiting healthy children for a controversial experiment in which researchers hope to make short children taller by injecting them with genetically engineered human growth hormone (HGH). Among other things, the researchers want to determine whether extra growth hormone does indeed make a child grow taller or just faster. Of 4 million children born in the U. S. every year, 90,000 will be in the bottom 3% in height. Some experts are troubled because it is the first time the NIH has exposed healthy children to medical risk for the sake of research, and this project treats a child's height—so often a matter of emotional bias, peer pressure or parental vanity—as a medical disability. Researchers are enrolling 80 volunteers who will be given injections three times a week for up to seven years. Dr. David L. Rimoin, an expert on short stature and pediatric growth disorders at Cedar-Sinai Medical Center in Los Angeles, characterizes this as a growth industry. NIH officials say that if fears about long-range side effects are laid to rest, the commercial market for human growth hormone could be as large as $4 billion a year.

INDIVIDUAL ISSUES	strongly agree	agree	not sure	disagree	strongly disagree
1. Parents have the right to provide their child with the enhanced opportunities that are offered by increased height.	❑	❑	❑	❑	❑
2. A parent should not give permission for a healthy child to be part of this study.	❑	❑	❑	❑	❑
3. A physician should be willing to urge parents to enroll their children in this study.	❑	❑	❑	❑	❑
4. A parent should invest the therapeutic money in counseling to help the child integrate who and what she is into a healthy self-image, rather than give her drugs.	❑	❑	❑	❑	❑
5. Using growth hormone to enhance height is no different than cosmetic surgery to enhance physical appearance.	❑	❑	❑	❑	❑

INSTITUTIONAL ISSUES

	strongly agree	agree	not sure	disagree	strongly disagree
1. Schools should deal more directly and extensively with cultural prejudices, such as bias against short persons.	❑	❑	❑	❑	❑
2. Health professionals should direct parents to psychological and social remedies for shortness, not drugs.	❑	❑	❑	❑	❑
3. The press should explore both the positive and negative medical and social aspects of this NIH study.	❑	❑	❑	❑	❑
4. The AMA should develop guidelines for experimentation with healthy children.	❑	❑	❑	❑	❑
5. Churches should help their congregations reflect on the morality of experimenting with children's height.	❑	❑	❑	❑	❑

SOCIETAL ISSUES

	strongly agree	agree	not sure	disagree	strongly disagree
1. The profit motive plays a disproportionate role in shaping the use of this drug.	❑	❑	❑	❑	❑
2. Manipulating our children's height in this way will not serve the best interests of future generations.	❑	❑	❑	❑	❑
3. Success in this project could dramatically change the complexion of the National Basketball Association. That would be valuable.	❑	❑	❑	❑	❑
4. The resources spent here should better be spent improving the scandalous status of polio vaccination in our country.	❑	❑	❑	❑	❑
5. The NIH needs to help the U. S. public recognize the value of such medical progress for future generations.	❑	❑	❑	❑	❑

#13: CLONING HUMAN EMBRYOS

Dr. Jerry Hall, at the fertilization program at George Washington University, successfully cloned human embryos. He divided 17 human embryos into 48 separate clusters of cells which survived for six days, when he discarded them. (Each of the 17 original embryos was abnormal and could not have survived to term.) This technique has been successfully used with animals for a long time. It was applied to humans as a way of giving infertile couples a better chance to conceive artificially by producing extra embryos. The George Washington University program has no intention of going any further with this experimentation. The director indicated that it is time to step back and think about what science has wrought. "I believe," he said "that what can come from this is a debate in the science, medical and ethics community." The news of this successful cloning has indeed unleashed a storm of controversy.

The American Fertility Society said that "this subject is of such grave importance that relevant guidelines should be established at the national level." Dr. Norman Fost, MD, an ethicist, disagreed. He said that he believed it was the parents' prerogative to decide what to do with their embryos. He starts with a presumption of privacy and liberty, and the belief that people should be able to live their lives the way they want and to make babies the way they want. Arthur Caplan, PhD, an ethicist, said that because cloning raises social issues, "there is room for governmental and societal debate and, perhaps, prohibitions and control and restraints."

INDIVIDUAL ISSUES	strongly agree	agree	not sure	disagree	strongly disagree
1. Persons have a right to privacy where reproduction is concerned.	❏	❏	❏	❏	❏
2. I have religious reasons for rejecting such reproduction.	❏	❏	❏	❏	❏
3. I would be willing to have children in this way if necessary.	❏	❏	❏	❏	❏
4. Dr. Hall should continue to improve this means of helping infertile persons.	❏	❏	❏	❏	❏
5. We should exercise extreme caution on this issue because we do not know the possible negative consequences for children conceived in this way.	❏	❏	❏	❏	❏

INSTITUTIONAL ISSUES

	strongly agree	agree	not sure	disagree	strongly disagree
1. The American Fertility Society has no ethical expertise to speak on such issues.	❑	❑	❑	❑	❑
2. Religious leaders have moral insight to guide the community on this issue.	❑	❑	❑	❑	❑
3. Hospitals should promote education of the public on such issues.	❑	❑	❑	❑	❑
4. High schools should make the discussion of such questions part of secondary education.	❑	❑	❑	❑	❑
5. The American Nurses Association should develop a position on the ethical acceptability of such experimentation.	❑	❑	❑	❑	❑

SOCIETAL ISSUES

	strongly agree	agree	not sure	disagree	strongly disagree
1. The burden of proof rests on anyone wanting to move forward with these experiments.	❑	❑	❑	❑	❑
2. In a market-driven culture like ours, the profit motive will drive too much of such an effort.	❑	❑	❑	❑	❑
3. Such interventions can only lead us to expect too much control over our destiny and our offspring.	❑	❑	❑	❑	❑
4. The government should provide funding for continued research on this project.	❑	❑	❑	❑	❑
5. Investing significant resources in such projects when we are still 20th in the world for infant mortality is a misallocation of resources.	❑	❑	❑	❑	❑

#14: AFFIRMATIVE ACTION

Fred was a remarkable young man. He had a strong sense of justice and concern for those who were less advantaged than himself. As a young man he had marched for civil rights. He often spoke out against what he saw as injustices toward women in his church and at his school. He aspired to being a doctor so that he could help others, possibly serving in the poor sections of urban America or the undeserved stretches of rural America.

Fred was a hard worker, but not an outstanding student. When he applied to his state's school of medicine, he was among those many who are qualified but not much more. He received a letter of rejection. His cousin, who worked in the office of admissions, told him that he was the victim of government requirements for affirmative action. Women and minority males who scored at his level were preferred to him because they had the "plus" of gender and race on their ledger. It was clear to Fred that he had little or no chance of admission to private or out-of-state medical schools if he could not make it in his home state. So he decided to go into social work, which also offered him the chance to help others.

INDIVIDUAL ISSUES	strongly agree	agree	not sure	disagree	strongly disagree
1. Fred has a right to be judged by his merits, not his race or gender.	❑	❑	❑	❑	❑
2. If Fred has not wronged someone, he has no debt to make restitution to them in this way.	❑	❑	❑	❑	❑
3. It is unfair that Fred's race and gender should be a liability to him—this is reverse discrimination.	❑	❑	❑	❑	❑
4. A minority person has more of a right to admission than Fred does.	❑	❑	❑	❑	❑
5. Fred should accept this sacrifice for the sake of others' advancement.	❑	❑	❑	❑	❑

INSTITUTIONAL ISSUES

	strongly agree	agree	not sure	disagree	strongly disagree
1. The medical school should not be a tool of social experimentation.	❏	❏	❏	❏	❏
2. The medical school should have a reasonable program of preferential admissions for minorities and women.	❏	❏	❏	❏	❏
3. The medical school should lobby to abolish such governmental interference.	❏	❏	❏	❏	❏
4. Such activity violates the mission of a school of medicine.	❏	❏	❏	❏	❏
5. A school can do more to abolish discrimination by teaching about fairness than by engaging in such social control.	❏	❏	❏	❏	❏

SOCIETAL ISSUES

	strongly agree	agree	not sure	disagree	strongly disagree
1. The Supreme Court should declare such programs unconstitutional.	❏	❏	❏	❏	❏
2. The Supreme Court has declared such efforts constitutionally acceptable.	❏	❏	❏	❏	❏
3. Such programs should be mandated in all professional schools and workplaces.	❏	❏	❏	❏	❏
4. Characterizing this as a "quota system" misrepresents the nature and effectiveness of affirmative action as a mechanism of social change.	❏	❏	❏	❏	❏
5. Mandating affirmative action programs is a misuse of government power and resources.	❏	❏	❏	❏	❏

#15: CHRISTIAN SCIENCE

Mrs. D. was a resident in a long-term care facility. She was a Christian Scientist for all of her adult life. She had been kind, peaceful, and a pleasure to be with. But lately her attitude and behavior were changing progressively. She was becoming suspicious, paranoid, and at times physically aggressive. Her treating physician's prognosis was that she would become progressively worse. Her condition could be treated with relative certainty and ease with psychotropic medication. But she had in the past clearly refused medication for other health problems by stating: "I've not taken a pill in over 80 years and I won't start now." In the judgment of the physician and other staff, she is no longer capable of making a decision, and they only have such history to work with. After Mrs. D physically attacked another elderly patient, one of the staff insisted that medicating her was less of an indignity than isolating her, locking her up, or physically restraining her. The staff was divided on how to best respect Mrs. D's dignity.

INDIVIDUAL ISSUES	strongly agree	agree	not sure	disagree	strongly disagree
1. Mrs. D's wishes are clearly known for this situation.	❑	❑	❑	❑	❑
2. Mrs. D has a right not to be medicated.	❑	❑	❑	❑	❑
3. Other residents have a right to have Mrs. D removed from their living space.	❑	❑	❑	❑	❑
4. Giving her medication would be the least indignity at this point in her life.	❑	❑	❑	❑	❑
5. There can be no grounds for giving her medication.	❑	❑	❑	❑	❑

INSTITUTIONAL ISSUES

	strongly agree	agree	not sure	disagree	strongly disagree
1. The institution should have a clear policy that religious preferences are honored, no matter what.	❑	❑	❑	❑	❑
2. The institution should have consistent staff education and discussion of such issues.	❑	❑	❑	❑	❑
3. The institution should do whatever it takes to make her life as pleasant as possible, regardless of her wishes or its own policy.	❑	❑	❑	❑	❑

	strongly agree	agree	not sure	disagree	strongly disagree
4. The institution should have a mechanism for providing surrogate decision-making in such situations.	❏	❏	❏	❏	❏
5. Without outside perspectives, the institution is likely to act in its own self-interest in resolving such questions.	❏	❏	❏	❏	❏

SOCIETAL ISSUES

	strongly agree	agree	not sure	disagree	strongly disagree
1. Society cannot be too careful in protecting the rights of patients in such settings.	❏	❏	❏	❏	❏
2. Harsh penalties should punish the violation of resident rights in such situations.	❏	❏	❏	❏	❏
3. There are too few resources dedicated to long-term care facilities in order to treat such situations adequately.	❏	❏	❏	❏	❏
4. To meet such needs of the elderly, our society should allocate more resources to long-term care.	❏	❏	❏	❏	❏
5. An increase in long-term care funds should come from limits set on acute care and not simply from taking more of the GNP for health care.	❏	❏	❏	❏	❏

#16: GOVERNOR'S HEART-LIVER TRANSPLANT

In June 1993 Robert P. Casey, the Governor of Pennsylvania, underwent an 18-hour transplant surgery in which he received both a heart and liver. A donor was found within 24 hours once doctors decided that the governor needed the emergency surgery. His condition was diagnosed two years earlier as amyloidosis, a hereditary disease that caused his liver to produce an abnormal protein that builds up on major organs. His heart and liver were so damaged by this disease that he was in danger of dying at any moment. A donated heart and liver came from a 34-year-old man from the Pittsburgh area. In the U.S., there are about 3000 persons waiting for liver transplants, of which 10+% will die before obtaining an organ.

INDIVIDUAL ISSUES	strongly agree	agree	not sure	disagree	strongly disagree
1. A governor deserves to be put at the head of the line.	❏	❏	❏	❏	❏
2. There should be no difference in access to such procedures, whether one is a governor or a homeless indigent.	❏	❏	❏	❏	❏
3. "First come, first served" should be our rule in allocating scarce organs.	❏	❏	❏	❏	❏
4. Organs are commodities and should be subjects to market dynamics.	❏	❏	❏	❏	❏
5. The governor should have refused to be treated in such a privileged way.	❏	❏	❏	❏	❏

INSTITUTIONAL ISSUES

	strongly agree	agree	not sure	disagree	strongly disagree
1. Such drastic measures are experimental, and insurance companies should not pay for them.	❏	❏	❏	❏	❏
2. The hospital should have stood by principle and made the governor wait his turn.	❏	❏	❏	❏	❏
3. The press should publish stories about the persons who died because they were passed over to benefit the governor.	❏	❏	❏	❏	❏
4. Hospitals should dampen, not fuel, the burning desire for ever-bolder rescue interventions.	❏	❏	❏	❏	❏

	strongly agree	agree	not sure	disagree	strongly disagree

5. Religion should have a neutral attitude toward such surgery. ☐ ☐ ☐ ☐ ☐

SOCIETAL ISSUES

1. In a world of limits, our society cannot afford such extravagance. ☐ ☐ ☐ ☐ ☐

2. The fairest way for society to allocate such organs is by lottery. ☐ ☐ ☐ ☐ ☐

3. By giving prominence to such attempts, we deepen the death-denying character of American culture. ☐ ☐ ☐ ☐ ☐

4. As a nation we would be better served to invest our health care dollars in prevention than in such rescue attempts. ☐ ☐ ☐ ☐ ☐

5. Our social policy should promote such efforts since they push back the frontiers of curative medicine. ☐ ☐ ☐ ☐ ☐

#17: THE BASIS OF FATHERHOOD

Glen Schwartz is an attorney in Los Angeles who specializes in "nonbiological father" cases. Mr. Schwartz has persuaded several judges to recognize such men's parental claims to children who aren't their natural or adoptive offspring. There is the case of an LA banker, Mr. McClinden, who lived with a woman for three years. A child was born during this time. After they broke up, she surprised him with the news that "their" two-year-old son, Scott, was not his biological child after all. Subsequent tests confirmed that Scott's natural father was a Mr. Smith. Mr. McClinden went to court and won paternity rights, prevailing over the claims of the mother, her new husband and the boy's natural father, Mr. Smith. Now that we have new biological options and social varieties of fatherhood, what should we do when one form of fatherhood conflicts with another form? Is there a trump among the varieties of fatherhood?

INDIVIDUAL ISSUES	strongly agree	agree	not sure	disagree	strongly disagree
1. A biological father has first and deepest claim on his genetic child.	❑	❑	❑	❑	❑
2. Fatherhood is most fundamentally a question of nurturing relationship.	❑	❑	❑	❑	❑
3. Fatherhood must be determined according to society's rules, laws, contracts.	❑	❑	❑	❑	❑
4. Fatherhood in such a case should be determined from the child's perspective—who, in the *child's experience*, is its father?	❑	❑	❑	❑	❑
5. In such cases the biological mother should have far more to say about a newborn than the biological father.	❑	❑	❑	❑	❑

INSTITUTIONAL ISSUES

	strongly agree	agree	not sure	disagree	strongly disagree
1. Schools should challenge the next generation to think about such issues long before they do it.	❑	❑	❑	❑	❑
2. Churches should spend more time considering such issues with their people.	❑	❑	❑	❑	❑
3. Churches should be active in lobbying for better legislation on such issues.	❑	❑	❑	❑	❑

	strongly agree	agree	not sure	disagree	strongly disagree
4. Professional schools—law, medicine, social work, etc.—should require that students spend time clarifying such issues for themselves.	❑	❑	❑	❑	❑
5. Hospitals should help their staffs think more deeply about such issues.	❑	❑	❑	❑	❑

SOCIETAL ISSUES

	strongly agree	agree	not sure	disagree	strongly disagree
1. Our laws should establish genetic parenthood as the basis for resolving such questions.	❑	❑	❑	❑	❑
2. Legislation is a poor societal method for dealing with such questions.	❑	❑	❑	❑	❑
3. We need much more than legislation if our society is to deal with such issues.	❑	❑	❑	❑	❑
4. Law should settle such cases based on a child's best interest.	❑	❑	❑	❑	❑
5. Law should declare that person the child's father who has most acted like a father to the child.	❑	❑	❑	❑	❑

#18: DOCTORS LOBBY PATIENTS

As the healthcare reform debate heats up, physicians are becoming more involved. For example, Ron Bronow, MD, gives his patients a form, requesting: "I'd like you to sign this, and if you have any questions I'll be happy to answer them." The form will be sent to the White House, and it says: "I don't want to be forced into managed care that will not allow freedom of choice in my selection of all my doctors. Please make sure that private practice medicine has the same opportunities as managed care in the final health care reform package." Dr. Bronow and his fellow members of Physicians Who Care, a group dedicated to the preservation of private practice, have gathered over 30,000 signatures in this way. They see this as an effort to practice patient advocacy and consider it their duty to alert and rally patients—for the patients' best interests. Many physicians agree and are beginning to offer political as well as medical advice. They know that they can no longer stand on the sidelines of politics but have a civic duty to join in and help their patients see the personal implications of public policy.

INDIVIDUAL ISSUES	strongly agree	agree	not sure	disagree	strongly disagree
1. Dr. Bronow should not do this.	❏	❏	❏	❏	❏
2. Dr. Bronow is misusing his position of professional power.	❏	❏	❏	❏	❏
3. Many patients will go along with the doctor's request out of fear of alienating their physician.	❏	❏	❏	❏	❏
4. This is no different from a physician asking patients to support programs for child health.	❏	❏	❏	❏	❏
5. If a patient refuses to cooperate, this could subtly change the physician's attitude toward this patient—for the worse.	❏	❏	❏	❏	❏

INSTITUTIONAL ISSUES

	strongly agree	agree	not sure	disagree	strongly disagree
1. The AMA should oppose such physician behavior.	❏	❏	❏	❏	❏
2. The AMA is behaving in ways that are more self-interested than this example.	❏	❏	❏	❏	❏
3. Health professionals should go beyond such a defense of the status quo.	❏	❏	❏	❏	❏

	strongly agree	agree	not sure	disagree	strongly disagree
4. Health professionals should lobby in public forums, but not in their offices.	❑	❑	❑	❑	❑
5. Health professionals know health care better than any other segment of the population. Such activity flows from that deeper knowledge.	❑	❑	❑	❑	❑

SOCIETAL ISSUES

	strongly agree	agree	not sure	disagree	strongly disagree
1. Public policy should recognize this as a clear conflict-of-interest activity.	❑	❑	❑	❑	❑
2. Such behavior should be illegal.	❑	❑	❑	❑	❑
3. The only antidote to such activity is a broad social-educational campaign.	❑	❑	❑	❑	❑
4. Society should consider this just another instance of informed consent.	❑	❑	❑	❑	❑
5. The right of physicians to express their opinion should be vigorously protected.	❑	❑	❑	❑	❑

#19: RU-486

In 1987, Étienne-Émile Baulieu, MD, the inventor of RU-486, said he hoped to see the day when women could buy the drug over the counter. Since then, he has changed his mind and is disturbed by the idea of "abortion by prescription." Too many things could go wrong if the French abortion pill is take without strict physician supervision and in tightly controlled settings.

RU-486 offers an alternative to surgical abortion. Since the pill was first marketed in France in 1988 by Roussel-Uclaf, mifepristone has been available only under tightly controlled conditions in a limited number of clinics in France, England, and Sweden. By early 1993, about 150,000 women have had abortions with RU-486. About 100,000 of those were in France, where 25% to 30% of women seeking abortions choose RU-486 over surgical abortions. RU-486 abortions in France are performed up to 49 days after the first day of the patient's last menstrual period; they can be done slightly later in England and Sweden. Dr. Andre Ulman, head of international development and marketing for the drug, reported in the *New England Journal* that RU-486 has an overall efficacy rate of 96% when used with a prostaglandin. French trials have not shown side effects more serious than those caused by surgical abortion. But RU-486 can cause incomplete abortions or hemorrhaging, and the accompanying prostaglandin can pose severe dangers, even death, to at-risk women.

Dr. Poppema, who owns an abortion clinic in Seattle and trained in France in the use of the drug, stressed the need for follow-up care because "complications of RU-486 are virtually the same in terms of bleeding and retained tissue as in a surgical abortion." But she reports that in her clinical experience only about 30-40% of patients return for follow-up. In France abortions are tightly supervised; in the U.S., once the FDA approves a drug, any licensed physician generally can prescribe it.

INDIVIDUAL ISSUES	strongly agree	agree	not sure	disagree	strongly disagree
1. Women have the right to have access to RU-486.	❏	❏	❏	❏	❏
2. To restrict RU-486 is unjust to women because it restricts their right to reproductive control.	❏	❏	❏	❏	❏
3. A physician should not prescribe RU-486 unless s/he can provide needed surgical back-up for all likely problems.	❏	❏	❏	❏	❏

	strongly agree	agree	not sure	disagree	strongly disagree
4. RU-486 represents a moral breakthrough because it corresponds so well to the private nature of abortion.	❑	❑	❑	❑	❑
5. A physician should make his/her voice heard in the public discussion about the availability of RU-486.	❑	❑	❑	❑	❑

INSTITUTIONAL ISSUES

1. Professional societies should resist introduction of RU-486 because of its many risks.	❑	❑	❑	❑	❑
2. Churches should make strong public efforts to restrict the number of abortions by opposing the availability of RU-486.	❑	❑	❑	❑	❑
3. Catholic bishops were right to hire a public relations firm to help convince the public of abortion's evils.	❑	❑	❑	❑	❑
4. Hospitals should assure strong informational programs about RU-486 since they will inevitably be involved in its consequences.	❑	❑	❑	❑	❑
5. Schools should educate their students about the public and private aspects of abortion.	❑	❑	❑	❑	❑

SOCIETAL ISSUES

1. Such an easy way to end fetal life will further erode social protection of the unborn.	❑	❑	❑	❑	❑
2. FDA must demand stringent studies before approving the drug.	❑	❑	❑	❑	❑
3. France's policy of restricting the use of RU-486 to strictly controlled clinic settings is more acceptable than simply allowing doctors to give prescriptions in a private office setting.	❑	❑	❑	❑	❑
4. RU-486 places abortion precisely where it belongs—in the privacy of the doctor-patient relationship.	❑	❑	❑	❑	❑
5. Abortion in pill form will further lead to the trivialization of abortion.	❑	❑	❑	❑	❑

#20: TEACHING ABOUT HOMOSEXUALITY

There is a new curriculum for New York City first-graders. Its purpose is to foster respect for all races, ethnic groups, and religions. So far, no controversy. But it also intends to encourage first-graders to "view lesbians/gays as real people to be respected and appreciated." It proposes that teachers offer several readings to promote such understanding. Suggested are: *Daddy's Roommate,* along with *Heather Has Two Mommies,* and *Gloria Goes to Gay Pride.* This part of the curriculum has caused heated controversy. New York's chancellor, Joseph Fernandez, insists that "It is very important that children learn early on that there are different family structures out there than the traditional one." Mary Cummins, board president of District 24, labeled portions of the study guide "dangerously misleading homosexual/lesbian propaganda."

INDIVIDUAL ISSUES	strongly agree	agree	not sure	disagree	strongly disagree
1. "We don't choose our sexual orientation, it chooses us."	❑	❑	❑	❑	❑
2. Sexual orientation is primarily a moral choice of an individual.	❑	❑	❑	❑	❑
3. Sexual orientation is probably a matter of biological inheritance.	❑	❑	❑	❑	❑
4. Sexual orientation is probably a product of social/psychological environment.	❑	❑	❑	❑	❑
5. Homosexuality is a life-style choice that persons should be free to make.	❑	❑	❑	❑	❑

INSTITUTIONAL ETHICS

	strongly agree	agree	not sure	disagree	strongly disagree
1. Schools should deal carefully, but directly, with the question of homosexuality.	❑	❑	❑	❑	❑
2. Churches should take a strong stand about respecting homosexuality.	❑	❑	❑	❑	❑
3. The home is the place where sexual orientation should be discussed.	❑	❑	❑	❑	❑
4. Sexual orientation should be part of school curriculum, but the first grade is too early.	❑	❑	❑	❑	❑
5. Schools should be clear that they do not condone homosexuality.	❑	❑	❑	❑	❑

SOCIETAL ETHICS

	strongly agree	agree	not sure	disagree	strongly disagree
1. We should have severe penalties for hate crimes, including gay-bashing.	❑	❑	❑	❑	❑
2. Society should not legalize homosexual marriage.	❑	❑	❑	❑	❑
3. No public money should be spent on the issue of homosexuality.	❑	❑	❑	❑	❑
4. Our civic communities should make special efforts to promote more understanding of and respect for gay men and lesbian women.	❑	❑	❑	❑	❑
5. American society has strong homophobic characteristics.	❑	❑	❑	❑	❑

#21: BABY JESSE'S HEART TRANSPLANT

In June 1986, 16-day-old baby Jesse received a heart transplant at Loma Linda University Medical Center to treat his fatal condition of hypoplastic left heart. While 80% of heart recipients experience rejection episodes, Jesse lived for seven years without such a crisis. But in 1993, Jesse's heart arteries began to narrow—threatening a heart attack. This is a side-effect that can occur in heart transplant, recipients of any age. A second transplant was provided in June 1993, but about a month later Jesse experienced severe rejection of this second transplant. Doctors were prepared to do a third transplant, but his condition deteriorated so badly they judged that his condition would not permit the procedure. Jesse was provided with comfort care, and died at age seven.

INDIVIDUAL ISSUES	strongly agree	agree	not sure	disagree	strongly disagree
1. Jesse had a right to his first transplant.	❑	❑	❑	❑	❑
2. Jesse should have had a chance for a second transplant.	❑	❑	❑	❑	❑
3. Jesse's life was worth whatever it cost.	❑	❑	❑	❑	❑
4. A physician should offer whatever treatments are available to parents in such a situation.	❑	❑	❑	❑	❑
5. If Jesse were my child, I would press for as many transplants as were feasible.	❑	❑	❑	❑	❑

INSTITUTIONAL ISSUES

	strongly agree	agree	not sure	disagree	strongly disagree
1. Loma Linda Hospital does a great service to the community by pushing back the frontiers of medicine.	❑	❑	❑	❑	❑
2. Schools should encourage organ donation as an altruistic and laudable act.	❑	❑	❑	❑	❑
3. It would be unfair for an insurance company to refuse to pay for such treatment.	❑	❑	❑	❑	❑
4. Schools should educate about the limits of health resources and the need for restraint in pursuing medical miracles.	❑	❑	❑	❑	❑
5. Once an institution has provided a transplant, they are committed to whatever care is needed to save the child's life.	❑	❑	❑	❑	❑

SOCIETAL ISSUES

	strongly agree	agree	not sure	disagree	strongly disagree
1. Since there are not enough transplants for everyone, no one should get a second one while another child dies for lack of a first one.	❏	❏	❏	❏	❏
2. When our nation has a national health program, we should fund such procedures for all children.	❏	❏	❏	❏	❏
3. We should change the law to allow us to harvest organs from anencephalic infants so we are able to provide organs for most children in need.	❏	❏	❏	❏	❏
4. We should dampen our zeal for transplantation and invest more health resources in other areas of care.	❏	❏	❏	❏	❏
5. We should spend more on transplants and open this possibility to children in foreign countries.	❏	❏	❏	❏	❏

#21: CHRISTIAN SCIENCE/HEALTH CARE

On August 26, 1993, in the first verdict of its kind, a jury has ordered the Christian Science Church to pay $9 million in punitive damages over the death of a boy whose mother, a member of the church, relied on prayer to treat his diabetes. The week before, the jury awarded the boy's father $5.2 million in compensatory damages from the Church, his former wife (the boy's mother), and her current husband. The boy, Ian Lundman, 11, died in 1989 after falling into a diabetic coma. His father said that the boy could have been saved if he had received medical treatment even two hours before his death. It seems that the jury tried to send a message to the Church to change its stand on spiritual healing where children are involved. The jury forewoman remarked: "The real issue for me was that a child didn't have a choice. I don't think it was about practicing religion; it was more about providing health care."

INDIVIDUAL ISSUES	strongly agree	agree	not sure	disagree	strongly disagree
1. Parents should be allowed to make all health care decisions for their children without external interference.	❏	❏	❏	❏	❏
2. When it's a question of life and death, the preservation of the child's life should be the deciding consideration.	❏	❏	❏	❏	❏
3. Religious freedom is so important that we must preserve it, even if it risks such rare loss of life.	❏	❏	❏	❏	❏
4. The loss of this child's life is tragic, but we should accept it as an inevitable consequence of a pluralistic society.	❏	❏	❏	❏	❏
5. Allowing such behavior confuses religious fanaticism with religious freedom.	❏	❏	❏	❏	❏

INSTITUTIONAL ISSUES

	strongly agree	agree	not sure	disagree	strongly disagree
1. The Christian Science Church should encourage parents to seek medical life-saving treatments for their children in such cases.	❏	❏	❏	❏	❏
2. Hospitals should seek to better understand the teachings of the Christian Science Church.	❏	❏	❏	❏	❏

	strongly agree	agree	not sure	disagree	strongly disagree

3. Hospitals should support legislation to avoid such treatment of children by Christian Science parents.

  ❑ ❑ ❑ ❑ ❑

4. Secondary schools should engage students in discussions of such cases.

  ❑ ❑ ❑ ❑ ❑

5. The Christian Science Church should stand by its conscience on these questions.

  ❑ ❑ ❑ ❑ ❑

SOCIETAL ISSUES

1. There should be a law requiring that parents follow the community standard of health care for their children, regardless of their religious beliefs.

  ❑ ❑ ❑ ❑ ❑

2. It is unfair for our society to deny children health care, on the one hand, and prosecute parents who refuse care out of religious conviction, on the other.

  ❑ ❑ ❑ ❑ ❑

3. There should be no attempt to formulate statutory law on this issue.

  ❑ ❑ ❑ ❑ ❑

4. The law should uphold parents' right to practice religion, even if it means that a few children might die as a result.

  ❑ ❑ ❑ ❑ ❑

5. To interfere with parents on this issue is inconsistent with our nation's position on abortion.

  ❑ ❑ ❑ ❑ ❑

#22: AGING POPULATION

There has been a steady decline in mortality between 1900 to the mid-1960s. At this point it appeared to plateau, and policymakers assumed that we had reached some genetically determined limit of life expectancy. But then it began again to decline to a marked degree. For example, from 1960 to 1988 life expectancy for U.S. women increased by 17.7% at age 65, 33.8% at age 85, but only 6.9% at birth. Since 1966, old-age mortality has decline steadily and will continue to do so into the next century. Among babies born 50 years ago, only 30% would have survived to their 65th birthday, while almost 80% of babies born today will live past their 65th birthday. But until more progress is made in understanding the causes and potential prevention of the disabilities of old age, increasing longevity will bring greater years of disability. The successful treatment of fatal diseases has transformed them into chronic diseases. The financial implications are formidable. Current costs for patients with moderate to severe dementia are estimated to be $35.5 billion per year. Conservative projections of five million cases of dementia in 2010 would result in costs of at least $80 billion (in 1985 dollars).

INDIVIDUAL ISSUES	strongly agree	agree	not sure	disagree	strongly disagree
1. Each of us should set limits to what we expect from the health care system.	❑	❑	❑	❑	❑
2. Filling out a durable power of attorney would take care of many problems concerning care of the elderly.	❑	❑	❑	❑	❑
3. Once I have lived a full life, I have a duty to make way for future generations.	❑	❑	❑	❑	❑
4. I have a right to the state-of-the-art health care procedures.	❑	❑	❑	❑	❑
5. If I become severely demented, I want all life-sustaining care to stop.	❑	❑	❑	❑	❑

INSTITUTIONAL ISSUES

	strongly agree	agree	not sure	disagree	strongly disagree
1. Churches should develop positions on care of the demented.	❑	❑	❑	❑	❑
2. Churches should recognize that respect for life does not exclude setting reasonable limits to care of the elderly.	❑	❑	❑	❑	❑

	strongly agree	agree	not sure	disagree	strongly disagree
3. Churches should lobby for more funds to be allocated for long-term care.	❑	❑	❑	❑	❑
4. Acute care institutions should set limits to their demands so that more resources are available for growing chronic care needs.	❑	❑	❑	❑	❑
5. Insurance companies would be justified in limiting payments for treatment of the severely demented elderly.	❑	❑	❑	❑	❑

SOCIETAL ISSUES

	strongly agree	agree	not sure	disagree	strongly disagree
1. If we deal with abuse, greed, and useless treatment, we have the resources to provide care for everyone.	❑	❑	❑	❑	❑
2. Our laws should allow us to end the lives of the severely demented if that was their wish when they were competent.	❑	❑	❑	❑	❑
3. Public policy should recognize that severe dementia can be worse than death.	❑	❑	❑	❑	❑
4. Spending $80 billion for the care of those with dementia is an appropriate use of health care resources.	❑	❑	❑	❑	❑
5. Only an integrated national system of health care can resolve such questions.	❑	❑	❑	❑	❑

#23: HOSPITALS MIRROR BIAS OF SOCIETY

Hospitals are often one of the major workplaces in a community. Ethical concerns arise not only in the treatment of patients but also in the organization of the workplace. Rosemary Stevens, in her historical study of the evolution of the U.S. hospital, *In Sickness and in Wealth,* (p. 357-8) says: "Hospital staffing is still a good reflection of contemporary class, gender, and racial relations—from the cadre of well-paid (still largely male) attending physicians, through the (largely female) ranks of nurses, therapists, and technicians, to the army of blue-collar workers in lesser-paid occupations, who are disproportionately members of minority groups."

INDIVIDUAL ISSUES	strongly agree	agree	not sure	disagree	strongly disagree
1. Changing such patterns should be the responsibility of the individuals in the institution.	❏	❏	❏	❏	❏
2. A manager should promote the very best person for a job without consideration of gender, race, etc.	❏	❏	❏	❏	❏
3. Women are less inclined to the rough and tumble required in higher management responsibilities.	❏	❏	❏	❏	❏
4. Due to their early experience, most minority persons cannot stand up to the demands of complex management.	❏	❏	❏	❏	❏
5. A woman who is promoted where there is a program of affirmative hiring and promotion will never feel she has earned the position.	❏	❏	❏	❏	❏

INSTITUTIONAL

	strongly agree	agree	not sure	disagree	strongly disagree
1. A hospital should have a program that gives special attention to the hiring of women.	❏	❏	❏	❏	❏
2. A hospital should examine the composition of its management personnel concerning women/minority representation.	❏	❏	❏	❏	❏
3. A hospital should examine the composition of its board of trustees concerning women/minority representation.	❏	❏	❏	❏	❏

	strongly agree	*agree*	*not sure*	*disagree*	*strongly disagree*

4. A hospital should programatically purchase a percentage of its goods/services from minority/women-owned businesses. ❏ ❏ ❏ ❏ ❏

5. There is no evidence that such programs do anything more than bloat the bureaucracy of an institution. ❏ ❏ ❏ ❏ ❏

SOCIETAL

1. The federal government should again become active in enforcing the regulations concerning women/minority hiring and promotion. ❏ ❏ ❏ ❏ ❏

2. Government-funded programs should insist on attention to gender/race in those institutions that receive federal funds. ❏ ❏ ❏ ❏ ❏

3. Quota programs are simplistic and punitive. ❏ ❏ ❏ ❏ ❏

4. Moral leadership is the answer to such questions, not the use of legal or political pressure. ❏ ❏ ❏ ❏ ❏

5. The racial and gender "problems" of our society are greatly exaggerated. ❏ ❏ ❏ ❏ ❏

#24: PHYSICIAN DATA DISCLOSURE

The states of New York and Pennsylvania were the first two states to release physician-specific health care data—both on bypass surgery outcomes. In Pennsylvania, the Health Care Cost Containment Council uses symbols to indicate where a given physician sits: a triangle means a doctor's outcomes were within an expected, risk-adjusted mortality range. Plus or minus signs are for those who did better or worse, respectively. On these released ratings will hang the reputations of doctors and the decision of patients about their own bypass surgeries. Other states are already considering the release of such data. Insurance companies and hospitals are expected to make use of such data for a myriad of their institutional decisions and practices.

INDIVIDUAL ISSUES	strongly agree	agree	not sure	disagree	strongly disagree
1. Patients have the right to know such vital information in order to make appropriate decisions.	❏	❏	❏	❏	❏
2. Doctors have a right to privacy until there is strong proof that such information is accurate and will be adequately understood and processed.	❏	❏	❏	❏	❏
3. This is merely the practical application of the principle of informed consent.	❏	❏	❏	❏	❏
4. Individual physicians should share such vital information within the physician-patient relationship, where it can be discussed and processed.	❏	❏	❏	❏	❏
5. Such an approach flows logically from a mentality of "health care providers" and "health care consumers."	❏	❏	❏	❏	❏

INSTITUTIONAL

	strongly agree	agree	not sure	disagree	strongly disagree
1. Hospitals should lobby that physicians be strongly involved in the gathering and utilization of such data.	❏	❏	❏	❏	❏
2. Hospitals should oppose such utilization of data.	❏	❏	❏	❏	❏

	strongly agree	agree	not sure	disagree	strongly disagree

3. AMA adopted principles for gathering and release of such information. This is a very important function of such professional organizations. ❑ ❑ ❑ ❑ ❑

4. Medical staffs should vigorously promote the collection and use of such data to improve institutional quality without making it public. ❑ ❑ ❑ ❑ ❑

5. Insurance companies should make use of such data in selecting physicians for their networks. ❑ ❑ ❑ ❑ ❑

SOCIETAL

1. The practice of gathering such data should be expanded to all major areas of medical practice. ❑ ❑ ❑ ❑ ❑

2. States should be guided by caution and careful planning of such efforts because of their potential for harm and misunderstanding. ❑ ❑ ❑ ❑ ❑

3. JCAHO should build appropriate use of such data into the credentialing process. ❑ ❑ ❑ ❑ ❑

4. This is a meat ax approach to legitimate social concerns that require the scalpel. ❑ ❑ ❑ ❑ ❑

5. Government should use legislative mechanisms to press for the appropriate use of such data. ❑ ❑ ❑ ❑ ❑

#25: SEVERELY HANDICAPPED NEWBORN

Michael S. was born to uninsured teen parents. He was born with ne-
crotic small bowel syndrome. This is ultimately a fatal condition, but
death can be postponed for months to years. Surgery determined there
was not enough bowel to allow him to take food in the normal way.
Hence, he had to be placed in a neonatal intensive care unit, where he
was fed by means of artificial nutrition. His ultimate prognosis is death
by the age of two due to liver failure from effects of the artificial nutrition. If he survives the full two years, his care will cost in excess of $1
million. The hospital where he was born has exclusive responsibility for
charity care in that community. If the hospital must absorb these costs,
then their emergency room must be closed to the poor, except for true,
life-threatening emergency cases.

INDIVIDUAL ISSUES	strongly agree	agree	not sure	disagree	strongly disagree
1. Michael's parents have a right to expect the community to provide care for their child.	❑	❑	❑	❑	❑
2. Michael's parents should allow Michael to die as peacefully and comfortably as possible.	❑	❑	❑	❑	❑
3. The attending physician should discourage the parents from aggressive treatments in this case.	❑	❑	❑	❑	❑
4. If Michael is not provided care, no other child with his condition should be provided with care.	❑	❑	❑	❑	❑
5. If Michael's parents can pay for Michael's care—through private insurance or out-of-pocket—it should be provided.	❑	❑	❑	❑	❑

INSTITUTIONAL ISSUES	strongly agree	agree	not sure	disagree	strongly disagree
1. An insurance company would act rightly if it refused to pay for such treatment.	❑	❑	❑	❑	❑
2. A hospital should have guidelines for allocating resources in such cases.	❑	❑	❑	❑	❑
3. A hospital's policy should be to treat such children if there is a chance of survival.	❑	❑	❑	❑	❑
4. A hospital's policy should be to provide the treatment that the parents decide is appropriate.	❑	❑	❑	❑	❑

	strongly agree	agree	not sure	disagree	strongly disagree

5. If Michael needs a liver transplant at age two to save his life, an insurance company should pay for it. ❑ ❑ ❑ ❑ ❑

SOCIETAL ISSUES

1. Michael would have been treated unjustly if he had been allowed to die and a well-insured infant with the same medical problems had been given full ICU care for two years. ❑ ❑ ❑ ❑ ❑

2. Oregon did a good job of deciding about society's providing such expensive care. ❑ ❑ ❑ ❑ ❑

3. There are 6,000 infants like Michael born each year in America. To be fair, a just and caring society must have a social policy that would provide aggressive life-sustaining care for all such infants or no such infants. ❑ ❑ ❑ ❑ ❑

4. It is better if we have no specific social policy at all with regard to infants like Michael, and simply allow private insurance companies to decide whether or not to cover infants like Michael. ❑ ❑ ❑ ❑ ❑

5. Even our wealthy nation needs to set limits to the health care it provides, and this case is one where we should deny care. ❑ ❑ ❑ ❑ ❑

#26: PARENTAL SMOKING AROUND CHILDREN

Over the past five years, there have been more than a dozen cases involving parental smoking in family courts around the country; in most, the judges have ruled against the parent who smoked. Almost all the cases so far involve children with health problems that are aggravated by smoke. In January 1993, the Environmental Protection Agency issued a report that found that secondhand smoke left children vulnerable to respiratory infections, ear infections and lung damage, and it estimates that environmental smoke caused as many as 300,000 cases of bronchitis or pneumonia and 26,000 cases of asthma in children every year.

In a current case in Contra Costa County, California, a woman is seeking an order preventing her former husband from smoking near his daughters, neither of whom has a respiratory disease. But many lawyers argue that the courts have no business interfering with legal behavior like smoking within the privacy of one's own home, especially if the children have no breathing problems. "It's extending the court too far into the family," said C. Clay Green, the lawyer representing the father in the Contra Costa County case. "The logical extension is that police should go into homes where parents smoke, whether or not they're divorcing."

INDIVIDUAL ISSUES	strongly agree	agree	not sure	disagree	strongly disagree
1. Parents should not smoke around their children, period.	❑	❑	❑	❑	❑
2. Every child has a right to a smoke-free home.	❑	❑	❑	❑	❑
3. A doctor has a duty to educate his/her patients about smoking harms to children.	❑	❑	❑	❑	❑
4. All parents expose their children to some risks—it's up to each parent to choose the risks and benefits of that household.	❑	❑	❑	❑	❑
5. A doctor should emphasize with the children of smokers the serious harms of secondhand smoke.	❑	❑	❑	❑	❑

	strongly agree	agree	not sure	disagree	strongly disagree
INSTITUTIONAL ISSUES					

INSTITUTIONAL ISSUES

1. Insurance companies should charge higher premiums for families with smokers. ❏ ❏ ❏ ❏ ❏

2. Churches should educate their congregations about the medical facts of smoking and children. ❏ ❏ ❏ ❏ ❏

3. Schools should give strong and repeated emphasis to the hazards of smoking. ❏ ❏ ❏ ❏ ❏

4. The AMA should make smoking one of its most visible and targeted enemies. ❏ ❏ ❏ ❏ ❏

5. The ACLU should campaign for the rights of parents to raise their children as they see fit. ❏ ❏ ❏ ❏ ❏

SOCIETAL ISSUES

1. If parents can be punished for smoking's harm to their children, so, too, with feeding their children too much fat in their diet. ❏ ❏ ❏ ❏ ❏

2. Smoking is a legal and accepted practice in this country and should remain an issue of private choice, not public policy. ❏ ❏ ❏ ❏ ❏

3. Society should come to recognize smoking around children as akin to medical neglect or a form of abuse. ❏ ❏ ❏ ❏ ❏

4. If our society can mandate car seats for children, we can outlaw smoking around children. ❏ ❏ ❏ ❏ ❏

5. Placing a $4 tax on each pack of cigarettes would go a long way to solving this problem. ❏ ❏ ❏ ❏ ❏

#27: CREATING A BALANCE AMONG HEALTHCARE SERVICES

Health care reform must address the issue of creating and maintaining a balance within health care services—acute, emergency, prevention, long-term, mental, dental, etc. We are currently far from this balanced allocation. A few examples in the area of mental health and supportive services can remind us of how often some services are dramatically underfunded compared to others.

L. A. County Jail has the largest mental health population of any single institution in the U.S. (over 3,500 inmates needing mental health services on any given day). There are more persons needing mental health services wandering the streets unhelped than there have been since before the Civil War.

Our children are being traumatized by witnessing violence more and more without a corresponding allocation of resources to treat the trauma/prevent its occurrence. *JAMA* (1/13/93) reports that:

- one in ten children attending Boston City Hospital pediatric clinic witnessed a shooting or stabbing—average age 2.7;

- a survey of elementary students in New Orleans showed over 90% had witnessed violence, 70% had seen a weapon used, 40% had seen a dead body.

- 10%-20% of homicides in Los Angeles are witnessed by children.

INDIVIDUAL ISSUES	strongly agree	agree	not sure	disagree	strongly disagree
1. I must be willing to expect fewer services and choices in my acute health care in order to provide expanded care in other areas— long-term, mental health, etc.	❏	❏	❏	❏	❏
2. A person with premier health care must be ready to have fewer choices in order for the 37 million without health care to be given access.	❏	❏	❏	❏	❏
3. Each one has a right to the health care that is provided as part of one's job or that one can pay for.	❏	❏	❏	❏	❏
4. My duties as a citizen include working for a better distribution of health care resources.	❏	❏	❏	❏	❏
5. The foundation of a healthy nation is that each person take responsibility for their own life choices—food, exercise, etc.	❏	❏	❏	❏	❏

INSTITUTIONAL ISSUES

	strongly agree	agree	not sure	disagree	strongly disagree
1. Our schools should spend far more time engaging students in consideration of an adequate health system.	❏	❏	❏	❏	❏
2. The media does more to promote ill health than all the germs on our continent.	❏	❏	❏	❏	❏
3. Hospitals should assume a more important role in the appropriate allocation of resources.	❏	❏	❏	❏	❏
4. Commercial television should change its ways and become a force in improving the allocation of our health resources.	❏	❏	❏	❏	❏
5. Physicians and nurses should be more involved in advocating for a balanced allocation of health resources.	❏	❏	❏	❏	❏

SOCIETAL ISSUES

	strongly agree	agree	not sure	disagree	strongly disagree
1. If we are to do justice to the mental health needs of our nation, we must invest substantially more resources in mental health services.	❏	❏	❏	❏	❏
2. To do this we will have to limit funds that are used for acute care.	❏	❏	❏	❏	❏
3. A wealthy nation like the U.S. can afford to care for those with mental health needs without curtailing other beneficial medical services.	❏	❏	❏	❏	❏
4. There is so much waste, duplication and fraud in the present system that we can finance much broader health services by eliminating these defects.	❏	❏	❏	❏	❏
5. The present patterns of allocation need only minor adjustments, not major reform.	❏	❏	❏	❏	❏

#28: ORGAN PROCUREMENT: PITTSBURGH

Transplant doctors say it is imperative that they move beyond brain-dead donors to find organs. Nearly 30,000 U.S. residents are on waiting lists for organs. There are only 10,000 to 12,000 brain deaths each year in the United States, and many of these patients are not suitable as donors because they are too old or because they fall into risk groups, e.g., for AIDS. A new group of donors could add a substantial number of candidates for organ donation— these are persons who are kept alive on life support but who request that this support be removed and their organs be donated after their heart stops beating. At the University of Pittsburgh, such patients are moved to a surgical suite where they are removed from the respirator with surgeons standing by to remove organs two minutes after the heart stops. Using this and other innovative techniques could increase the supply of organs by 25%.

INDIVIDUAL ISSUES	strongly agree	agree	not sure	disagree	strongly disagree
1. Such a procedure could give meaning to a patient's final days.	❑	❑	❑	❑	❑
2. A nurse should encourage patients to do this.	❑	❑	❑	❑	❑
3. I would want a loved one to consent to this procedure.	❑	❑	❑	❑	❑
4. Getting genuine informed consent for such a procedure will be very difficult.	❑	❑	❑	❑	❑
5. The dignity of human dying is at risk in this procedure, even if a patient gives consent.	❑	❑	❑	❑	❑

INSTITUTIONAL ISSUES

	strongly agree	agree	not sure	disagree	strongly disagree
1. The transplant movement should not be proud of this effort.	❑	❑	❑	❑	❑
2. A hospital should surround such a practice with strong safeguards for patient protection.	❑	❑	❑	❑	❑
3. A hospital should forbid such a practice.	❑	❑	❑	❑	❑
4. A hospital should submit such a program to intense and extended scrutiny by objective outside parties before beginning.	❑	❑	❑	❑	❑

	strongly agree	agree	not sure	disagree	strongly disagree

5. A hospital should treat such a procedure as an experiment with strong social/psychological data gathering and analysis. ❏ ❏ ❏ ❏ ❏

Societal Issues

1. Society should be concerned about what this will say to the next generation regarding death and dying. ❏ ❏ ❏ ❏ ❏

2. Such altruism will bind the community more closely. ❏ ❏ ❏ ❏ ❏

3. Saving thousands of lives justifies whatever social costs are involved. ❏ ❏ ❏ ❏ ❏

4. We would be better off with bold experiments in vaccinating all of our nation's children. ❏ ❏ ❏ ❏ ❏

5. This approach represents another step in making a person's life and death be measured by its *usefulness*. ❏ ❏ ❏ ❏ ❏

#29: PERFUSION BY PIG LIVER

Surgeons at Duke University used a succession of five pig livers to keep 22-year-old Eric Thomas alive until a human liver became available for transplant. His own liver had been destroyed by fulminent hepatitis B, and a donor liver could not be found for almost a week. In six-hour sessions on each of those days, blood from his femoral vein was circulated out of his body, through a pig liver, and back into his circulatory system. His blood was oxygenated by an extracorporeal membrane oxygenation device. Finally, a suitable donor liver was found and transplanted. He was discharged from the hospital on January 4, 1993 and is reportedly recovering well.

INDIVIDUAL ISSUES	strongly agree	agree	not sure	disagree	strongly disagree
1. The use of animals for human benefit, such as this case, is ethically a good thing.	❑	❑	❑	❑	❑
2. Mr. Thomas has a right to expect that the most recent possibilities of medicine are offered to him.	❑	❑	❑	❑	❑
3. Mr. Thomas should get such extraordinary treatment only if he can pay for it himself.	❑	❑	❑	❑	❑
4. A physician should not offer marginal medical options to desperate persons who can be coerced by their desperation.	❑	❑	❑	❑	❑
5. Desperate situations call for desperate measures.	❑	❑	❑	❑	❑

INSTITUTIONAL ISSUES					
1. Hospitals should press for funds to continue pushing back the frontiers of death.	❑	❑	❑	❑	❑
2. Professional societies should urge restraint in such practices.	❑	❑	❑	❑	❑
3. Animal rights groups should be active in monitoring such experimentation with animals.	❑	❑	❑	❑	❑
4. Hospitals should help the general public scale back its expectations of medical miracles as much as possible.	❑	❑	❑	❑	❑

	strongly agree	agree	not sure	disagree	strongly disagree
5. The press should help the general public have realistic expectations of medical care by clarifying the cost trade-offs of such highly expensive procedures.	❑	❑	❑	❑	❑

SOCIETAL

	strongly agree	agree	not sure	disagree	strongly disagree
1. In such matters of life and death, society's imperative must be in favor of saving life.	❑	❑	❑	❑	❑
2. A just health care system will provide such care for everyone or for no one.	❑	❑	❑	❑	❑
3. There should be tax incentives to bring research into such areas of medical progress.	❑	❑	❑	❑	❑
4. Health resources should be invested very sparingly in such projects.	❑	❑	❑	❑	❑
5. We should develop a process like Oregon did to prioritize such treatments relative to other procedures.	❑	❑	❑	❑	❑

#30: RATIO OF PRIMARY CARE TO SPECIALTY PHYSICIANS

Being a family physician appeals to fewer and fewer young doctors these days. The movement—flight?—from primary care to more specialized branches of medicine has been dramatic. In 1992 legislation was proposed in California to stem the flight of physicians from primary care—family medicine, pediatrics, OB/GYN. Assembly Bill 3593 would use financial incentives for medical schools to promote their cooperation in achieving the desired balance. AB 3593 would mandate that 50% of all graduates of the five University of California medical schools accept primary care residencies and that 20% of the total train as family physicians. Otherwise there would be substantial financial penalties to the schools in proportion to their failure to meet these parameters. Major arguments about such measures include:

- the overall cost of care for the community increases in direct proportion to the ratio of specialists to primary care physicians;
- accessibility of basic health care in the community depends on the ratio of primary care physicians to specialists;
- other nations contain health costs by regulating the ratio of primary care physicians to specialists issues surrounding civil rights and freedom of choice;
- issues surrounding preference/choice as basis for professional satisfaction and quality of care.

INDIVIDUAL ISSUES	strongly agree	agree	not sure	disagree	strongly disagree
1. This is primarily a question of freedom of choice. We can't suspend the Bill of Rights.	❏	❏	❏	❏	❏
2. Doctors will practice most effectively in those fields which have the most attraction for them.	❏	❏	❏	❏	❏
3. Doctors should be able to choose a field based on its potential income.	❏	❏	❏	❏	❏
4. It is an injustice when patients cannot access care because doctors are allowed to choose specialties.	❏	❏	❏	❏	❏
5. For the sake of patient care, medical students should be given maximal freedom in choosing their field of practice.	❏	❏	❏	❏	❏

INSTITUTIONAL ISSUES

	strongly agree	agree	not sure	disagree	strongly disagree
1. Medical schools should teach medicine, not be the instruments of social policy.	❑	❑	❑	❑	❑
2. Medical schools should recognize the wisdom of this approach and implement it.	❑	❑	❑	❑	❑
3. Medical schools should address this problem with their students as part of their medical education.	❑	❑	❑	❑	❑
4. Medical schools should work with the state legislature to create a reasonable solution to this problem.	❑	❑	❑	❑	❑
5. The press should help the public understand the key issues that are at stake in this question.	❑	❑	❑	❑	❑

SOCIETAL ISSUES

	strongly agree	agree	not sure	disagree	strongly disagree
1. Free market is the American way—here, too, it will provide the best approach.	❑	❑	❑	❑	❑
2. The legislature has no business in such issues of medical education.	❑	❑	❑	❑	❑
3. Taxpayers of California pay $226,000 for every specialist MD education. They should have a voice in how their tax money is spent.	❑	❑	❑	❑	❑
4. The long-range solution should include paying primary care physicians more and specialists less for their professional services.	❑	❑	❑	❑	❑
5. Society could save $50 billion annually by seeing to it that 50% of our physicians are primary care providers. We should take whatever steps are necessary to achieve this.	❑	❑	❑	❑	❑

#31: RESTRICT ORGANS FOR FOREIGNERS

In the summer of 1993, the U. S. Congress was considering a bill that would tighten laws on organ sharing. The proposed legislation would create two separate waiting lists for organs: the primary list would include U. S. citizens who need organs; the second, low-priority list would include foreigners who want to receive organs in the U. S. Only after the primary list was exhausted would anyone on the secondary list be eligible for an organ. This would effectively exclude foreigners from receiving organs in this country, since it is unlikely that enough organs would be available to cover all those on the primary list, much less a surplus for foreigners. Supporters of such legislation point out that other nations have allocation policies similar to the one now being considered. Current legislation limits non-U.S. resident transplants to 10% of a hospital transplant program's patients.

INDIVIDUAL ISSUES	strongly agree	agree	not sure	disagree	strongly disagree
1. Doctors should respond to persons who knock on the door for help, regardless of what passport they carry.	❑	❑	❑	❑	❑
2. Transplant surgeons should be more concerned with an overall fair system than they seem to be at present.	❑	❑	❑	❑	❑
3. Physicians need the privilege of focusing on the direct care of patients; developing institutional and social policy should fall to others.	❑	❑	❑	❑	❑
4. More clinical professionals should be bold in seeking donor organs from patients and families in order to mitigate the shortage of organs.	❑	❑	❑	❑	❑
5. More individuals should be willing to share their organs.	❑	❑	❑	❑	❑

INSTITUTIONAL ISSUES

	strongly agree	agree	not sure	disagree	strongly disagree
1. Hospitals should work for a better overall system of organ procurement and allocation.	❑	❑	❑	❑	❑
2. Television should help the general public better understand the issues at stake in this question.	❑	❑	❑	❑	❑

	strongly agree	agree	not sure	disagree	strongly disagree
3. Newspapers should spend more space on issues of prevention and less on recounting the "miracles" of rescue medicine.	❑	❑	❑	❑	❑
4. Churches should be active in lobbying for better public policy concerning transplants.	❑	❑	❑	❑	❑
5. Hospitals give the impression that they are more interested in promoting their own interests than in creating an overall fair system.	❑	❑	❑	❑	❑

SOCIETAL ISSUES

	strongly agree	agree	not sure	disagree	strongly disagree
1. To obtain more organs we should legalize presumed consent to harvest organs, like many other countries already do.	❑	❑	❑	❑	❑
2. On many questions of transplantation, we could learn much from foreign countries.	❑	❑	❑	❑	❑
3. I agree with the proposed new legislation restricting foreigners.	❑	❑	❑	❑	❑
4. We should stick with the 10% limit of current practice, but not become as restrictive as the new legislation proposes.	❑	❑	❑	❑	❑
5. The fairest way to allocate organs would be a lottery for all those with a clear medical need. Other policy attempts are ultimately unfair.	❑	❑	❑	❑	❑

#32: EXPANDED USE OF ADVANCED-PRACTICE NURSES

An important element of health care reform could be an expanded role for nurses. Between 1970 and 1990 the proportion of doctors in primary care declined rapidly, and the rate of decline is accelerating. One way to increase the access to primary care is to make greater use of advanced-practice nurses. The Yale Journal of Regulation summarized two decades of research on this question. The conclusions are that nurse practitioners and midwives prescribe fewer drugs, use fewer tests, and select lower-cost treatments and settings. Nevertheless, they can safely substitute for physicians for 90% of primary care needed for children and up to 80% required by adults. International comparisons suggest that at least 75% of all prenatal care and delivery of babies could be safely provided by nurse midwives. But in the U.S., nurses deliver less than 4% of births. The Yale report concluded that significant financial, legal, and professional structures prevent the effective use of nurses.

INDIVIDUAL ISSUES	strongly agree	agree	not sure	disagree	strongly disagree
1. I would welcome primary care for myself from a nurse practitioner.	❏	❏	❏	❏	❏
2. To expand the practice of nursing beyond its present parameters would be unsafe.	❏	❏	❏	❏	❏
3. A nurse would be more likely to serve in rural and urban underserved areas.	❏	❏	❏	❏	❏
4. A nurse with advanced training has a right to practice with fewer constraints than are currently present.	❏	❏	❏	❏	❏
5. Patients without access to primary care have a right to the services of an advanced-practice nurse.	❏	❏	❏	❏	❏

INSTITUTIONAL ISSUES					
1. Hospitals should familiarize their staffs with studies in this area.	❏	❏	❏	❏	❏
2. Hospital trustees should be educated concerning the expanded use of advanced-practice nurses.	❏	❏	❏	❏	❏
3. Medical staffs should accept advanced-practice nurses into their ranks.	❏	❏	❏	❏	❏

	strongly agree	agree	not sure	disagree	strongly disagree

4. Hospital ethics committees should raise these questions for the hospital community. ❑ ❑ ❑ ❑ ❑

5. The media should help the general public become more accepting of primary care by advanced-practice nurses. ❑ ❑ ❑ ❑ ❑

SOCIETAL ISSUES

1. Malpractice and tort reform should remove some barriers to expanded nursing practice that currently exist. ❑ ❑ ❑ ❑ ❑

2. Society should promote expanded use of advanced-practice nurses as a more reasonable and just allocation of resources. ❑ ❑ ❑ ❑ ❑

3. Medicare should be changed to give direct reimbursement to advanced-practice nurses. ❑ ❑ ❑ ❑ ❑

4. Hospitals should be required to offer admitting privileges to advanced-practice nurses as a condition of participation in Medicare and Medicaid. ❑ ❑ ❑ ❑ ❑

5. Bonus payments should be given to doctors and nurses who serve in underserved rural and urban areas. ❑ ❑ ❑ ❑ ❑

#33: DEFENSE INDUSTRY DIVERSITY

The federal government requires its contractors to diversify their work forces and their management. Under federal procurement rules, any company that receives a contract for $10,000 or more is required to undertake an affirmative action program to assure that women and minorities are given fair opportunity for employment and advancement. If contractors violate their agreement to move toward compliance, they are warned that they will be barred from doing business with the federal government. In fact, no contractor is known to have been so barred. Both the Reagan and Bush administrations were notably slow to enforce any diversity policies. Data provided by the nation's 10 largest weapons makers show that of the 2,612 executives listed as senior management, women made up 5.3% and minorities 4.8%. At Hughes Aircraft, for example—which appointed its first female and minority presidents in 1987—of 75 senior executives, 5 are women and 5 are members of minorities. The Lockheed Corporation made diversity a priority, and its number of women vice presidents increased to 20 from 13 in the last five years. Fifteen members of minorities are now vice presidents, up from nine. Joyce Miller, the newly appointed executive director of the Federal Commission on the Glass Ceiling said: "We know that there is a glass ceiling in almost every industry, and we will be formulating policies to help break through it."

INDIVIDUAL ISSUES	strongly agree	agree	not sure	disagree	strongly disagree
1. A woman or minority deserves such extra help in our present structures.	❑	❑	❑	❑	❑
2. Preference for you is discrimination against me.	❑	❑	❑	❑	❑
3. Only if I have been personally discriminated against do I have a claim to remedial action.	❑	❑	❑	❑	❑
4. Individuals are responsible for their own lives.	❑	❑	❑	❑	❑
5. "Two wrongs don't make a right" is an important principle in deciding such questions.	❑	❑	❑	❑	❑

INSTITUTIONAL ISSUES

	strongly agree	agree	not sure	disagree	strongly disagree
1. Institutions should establish remedial programs that address this question.	❑	❑	❑	❑	❑
2. An institution has done enough when it assures that it practices no deliberate discrimination.	❑	❑	❑	❑	❑
3. An organization that promotes such programs sends the wrong message: "You can't make it on your own!"	❑	❑	❑	❑	❑
4. The organization that I know best would do well to take remedial steps concerning women and minorities.	❑	❑	❑	❑	❑
5. Organizations should leave this alone; it is up to individuals to solve.	❑	❑	❑	❑	❑

SOCIETAL ISSUES

1. Our society is systemically biased against women.	❑	❑	❑	❑	❑
2. Our society is systemically biased against minorities.	❑	❑	❑	❑	❑
3. Public policy cannot avoid making this a quota issue, and that is unjust.	❑	❑	❑	❑	❑
4. The Reagan/Bush approach—go slow in enforcing policies—was correct.	❑	❑	❑	❑	❑
5. The evidence that such efforts make a difference should lead to more public policy efforts in this regard.	❑	❑	❑	❑	❑

#34: NORPLANT

Norplant consists of six matchstick-size capsules surgically implanted in the arm that slowly release a low dosage of levonorgestrel, the same synthetic hormone used in several versions of the birth-control pill. Norplant is as good as the pill in preventing pregnancy, and its long-lasting effectiveness—up to five years—makes it especially attractive to younger women who want to delay childbearing. It's teenager-proof; girls don't have to worry about remembering to take the pill or use a diaphragm. That's why the Paquin School in Baltimore is so high on Norplant. Paquin's 300 students are all pregnant teens or new mothers. In January 1993 these girls became the first students in the U. S. to be offered the implantable contraceptive at school. Gracie Dawkins, a Paquin counselor said: "Our dream is to prevent them from getting pregnant again until they're at least 21." But Melvin Tuggle, a black Baltimore minister, voices strong opposition to such use of Norplant. He comments: "In the Baltimore school system, a 12-year-old needs a letter from her parents to go to the zoo. She needs permission to get aspirin, but she needs nothing to get Norplant." Others, viewing the issue from the perspective of welfare, comment that if taxpayers support the children of the poor, they should have a say in whether the children will be conceived. To date, 13 states have proposed nearly two dozen bills that aim to use Norplant as an instrument of social policy. The bottom line for the principal of Paquin is simple: Norplant can offer young mothers a second chance to put their lives back on track.

INDIVIDUAL ISSUES	strongly agree	agree	not sure	disagree	strongly disagree
1. Providing adequate information in an appropriate environment for informed consent about Norplant is a central issue, but most difficult to achieve.	❏	❏	❏	❏	❏
2. At some point a woman loses her right to conceive more children.	❏	❏	❏	❏	❏
3. Offering young mothers a second chance is worth the other risks involved in such a program.	❏	❏	❏	❏	❏
4. Such a quick chemical fix to this question leads to further confusion about the meaning of sexuality.	❏	❏	❏	❏	❏
5. Any woman old enough to be pregnant is old enough to make a decision about Norplant.	❏	❏	❏	❏	❏

INSTITUTIONAL ISSUES

	strongly agree	agree	not sure	disagree	strongly disagree
1. By promoting Norplant, schools give the unavoidable impression that they are condoning promiscuity.	❏	❏	❏	❏	❏
2. Schools should teach abstinence, not give out Norplant.	❏	❏	❏	❏	❏
3. Norplant should be part of school programs only if it is part of a larger, well-planned effort.	❏	❏	❏	❏	❏
4. Schools should stick to education, and force other parts of society to take on their responsibility for such issues.	❏	❏	❏	❏	❏
5. If schools require parental permission for a field trip to the zoo, they should require parental permission for Norplant.	❏	❏	❏	❏	❏

SOCIETAL ISSUES

	strongly agree	agree	not sure	disagree	strongly disagree
1. A study in Texas indicated that many condom users would stop using condoms now that they have Norplant. We should remedy such problems before instituting the widespread use of Norplant.	❏	❏	❏	❏	❏
2. The most effective way to control fertility is by raising the standard of living, and that is where we should put our emphasis.	❏	❏	❏	❏	❏
3. For social policy the bottom line on Norplant is this: it can effectively prevent teenage pregnancies.	❏	❏	❏	❏	❏
4. We should see teenage pregnancy as a broad and deep social problem, and not be misled by such band-aid approaches as Norplant.	❏	❏	❏	❏	❏
5. Norplant cannot avoid becoming a tool of racist and classist policies.	❏	❏	❏	❏	❏

#35: HOME HEALTH CASE STUDY

Mrs. Smith is an 80-year-old single woman with no known relatives. She lives alone in a small apartment in a dangerous neighborhood. She is insulin-dependent, increasingly confused, has worsening eyesight, and is experiencing urinary incontinence. Due to concerns about their own safety and the conditions in which Mrs. Smith must live, two home care attendants have already refused to continue assignments to her. She needs 24-hour supervision. Medicaid may not certify this level of care. The agency staff responsible for her are pressing her to enter a nursing home. Mrs. Smith insists that she would rather die at home without care than enter a nursing home.

INDIVIDUAL ISSUES	strongly agree	agree	not sure	disagree	strongly disagree
1. Mrs. Smith has a right to remain in her home.	❑	❑	❑	❑	❑
2. Mrs. Smith has a right to receive decent care in her home.	❑	❑	❑	❑	❑
3. Mrs. Smith must face the realistic limits of her situation.	❑	❑	❑	❑	❑
4. Home care professionals have a right to refuse to care for Mrs. Smith.	❑	❑	❑	❑	❑
5. It seems Mrs. Smith needs others to make her healthcare decisions.	❑	❑	❑	❑	❑

INSTITUTIONAL ISSUES	strongly agree	agree	not sure	disagree	strongly disagree
1. The agency should use every means to convince her to move.	❑	❑	❑	❑	❑
2. The agency should find a way to care for her in her home.	❑	❑	❑	❑	❑
3. The agency should face the fact: it can't solve everybody's problem.	❑	❑	❑	❑	❑
4. The agency should provide insufficient care rather than no care at all.	❑	❑	❑	❑	❑
5. If the staff needs to bend the truth to get money for care, that is acceptable.	❑	❑	❑	❑	❑

SOCIETAL ISSUES

	strongly agree	agree	not sure	disagree	strongly disagree
1. Spending great sums of money for curative medicine while underfunding home health is a serious injustice.	❑	❑	❑	❑	❑
2. To finance home health, we should take funds from acute care.	❑	❑	❑	❑	❑
3. We can fund home care without cutting other health services.	❑	❑	❑	❑	❑
4. Health administrative costs (20-25% of current spending) should be severely cut to fund home care.	❑	❑	❑	❑	❑
5. Changing home health funding would hardly help a case like this.	❑	❑	❑	❑	❑

#36: HATE SPEECH

In Germany it is against the law to display the swastika, make the Nazi salute, and deny that the Holocaust took place. Minnesota passed a law that was similar in structure and intent. It banned cross-burning, the swastika and other symbols "which arouse anger, alarm, or resentment in others on the basis of race, color, creed, religion or gender." In June 1992, the U.S. Supreme Court struck down that Minnesota law. The court was upholding a widely affirmed view of U.S. society that true democracy requires that even the most repugnant and insulting ideas deserve a hearing—even if they gravely offend others. The U.S. seems to be saying that we trust the good sense of the populace. Germany seems to be saying that such good sense does not protect persons sufficiently from the wounds inflicted by hate speech—verbal or symbolic.

INDIVIDUAL ISSUES	strongly agree	agree	not sure	disagree	strongly disagree
1. Action should be restricted, but freedom of speech must be fiercely protected.	❑	❑	❑	❑	❑
2. Speech is clearly human action, often resulting in serious harm or benefit. Action does not only come in the form of caresses and punches.	❑	❑	❑	❑	❑
3. Our right to freedom of speech must be seen as virtually limitless.	❑	❑	❑	❑	❑
4. Even the most repugnant ideas must be allowed expression.	❑	❑	❑	❑	❑
5. Rather than drawing a line between speech and action, we should establish boundaries based on severity of harm done to other persons	❑	❑	❑	❑	❑

INSTITUTIONAL ISSUES

1. Universities should protect academic freedom and restrict speech in no way whatsoever.	❑	❑	❑	❑	❑
2. Work environments should set limits to offensive speech that goes beyond the boundaries of "sexual harassment."	❑	❑	❑	❑	❑
3. Education and moral persuasion, not regulations and sanctions, are better ways to deal with such issues.	❑	❑	❑	❑	❑

	strongly agree	agree	not sure	disagree	strongly disagree

4. The workplace should not attempt to control sexually offensive or any other form of offensive speech. ❏ ❏ ❏ ❏ ❏

5. The armed forces, workplaces, etc., should develop clear expectations and sanctions concerning acceptable talk. ❏ ❏ ❏ ❏ ❏

SOCIETAL ISSUES

1. Public policy should protect individuals from the harm of hate speech rather than protect the freedom of those who speak hatefully. ❏ ❏ ❏ ❏ ❏

2. We would be better off imitating Germany's approach and setting some clear, limited boundaries for gross violations. ❏ ❏ ❏ ❏ ❏

3. Sexual harassment in speech is precisely an example of prohibiting offensive speech—it should not be restricted to gender/sexual issues. ❏ ❏ ❏ ❏ ❏

4. Social science and practice has long recognized the deep and lasting harm of verbal abuse; hate speech legislation is a logical extension of such insight. ❏ ❏ ❏ ❏ ❏

5. We restrict freedom in polluting the atmosphere by restricting leaf-burning and auto emissions. We should also restrict social pollution of insulting speech. ❏ ❏ ❏ ❏ ❏

#37: JEHOVAH'S WITNESS AND CHILD

A staunch Jehovah's Witness, the mother of two small children, expected to have a difficult delivery of her third child. The obstetrician judged that vaginal delivery was not possible and that a C-section was necessary. Before the surgery, she had refused to sign a consent form for blood transfusion. The condition of the child required, in the judgment of the attending physicians, an immediate blood transfusion to save his life. When the parents refused permission for such treatment, a hearing was conducted by a judge and she ordered a guardian be appointed for the child who would sign the necessary releases. This occurred and the child was given the transfusions. While this was occurring, the mother began hemorrhaging and the physicians said that she needed an emergency hysterectomy and several units of blood to avert her death. The patient authorized the surgery but refused all blood transfusion. The judge refused to override the patient's wishes, no transfusion was given and the mother bled to death several hours later.

INDIVIDUAL ISSUES	strongly agree	agree	not sure	disagree	strongly disagree
1. The mother should have given permission for transfusions for her child.	❏	❏	❏	❏	❏
2. The mother should have given permission for transfusions for herself.	❏	❏	❏	❏	❏
3. Religious beliefs should prevail over clinical judgments.	❏	❏	❏	❏	❏
4. A surgeon should save life first and worry about the consequences later.	❏	❏	❏	❏	❏
5. Jehovah's Witnesses have no right to request the services of a surgeon if they tie one hand behind the surgeon's back.	❏	❏	❏	❏	❏

INSTITUTIONAL ISSUES

	strongly agree	agree	not sure	disagree	strongly disagree
1. Hospitals should have clear policies that protect the religious preferences of patients, no matter what these are.	❏	❏	❏	❏	❏
2. An institution would be justified in refusing to accept patients for treatment unless they were willing to accept standard medical care.	❏	❏	❏	❏	❏

	strongly agree	agree	not sure	disagree	strongly disagree
3. A hospital should train its staff to honor the wishes of patients, even if they seem strange and irrational.	❑	❑	❑	❑	❑
4. A hospital should respect the wishes of parents, even if this involves not giving their children certain medical treatments.	❑	❑	❑	❑	❑
5. A hospital should investigate and offer the full range of alternatives to blood transfusion that is now available.	❑	❑	❑	❑	❑

SOCIETAL ISSUES

1. The practice of the courts to insist on necessary transfusions for children is a good one.	❑	❑	❑	❑	❑
2. The courts should not allow mothers to risk making their children orphans by refusing blood transfusions.	❑	❑	❑	❑	❑
3. Society should consider this mother's refusal of blood for herself as a form of child abandonment.	❑	❑	❑	❑	❑
4. No society has a right to tell parents how to treat their children.	❑	❑	❑	❑	❑
5. Society should allow great freedom to families, but still be able to characterize such decisions as unreasonable and unacceptable.	❑	❑	❑	❑	❑

#38: PERSISTENT VEGETATIVE STATE

Mrs. P suffered a severe stroke that left her in a persistent vegetative state (PVS). This is a condition in which the higher brain center—which accounts for human awareness, feeling and expression—is destroyed permanently. But the brain stem—which accounts for some vegetative functions such as breathing and digestion—continues to function. Persons in such a state can survive for years and even decades, but there is no hope of them ever regaining consciousness. It is estimated that there are some 10,000 persons in the United States in this condition, with an annual cost of about $1.5 billion.

Once the hospital staff determined that Mrs. P was in PVS, they recommended that further curative and life-sustaining care be discontinued and only comfort care be provided. But her husband and children said that she was a fighter and had expressed the wish to have her life extended as long as possible. After further discussions with the family, and the family's continued insistence on full care, the hospital went to court in an effort to stop treatment that they considered unreasonable. When Mrs. P died she had been treated for over a year at a cost of more than $1,000,000 without her condition changing.

INDIVIDUAL ISSUES	strongly agree	agree	not sure	disagree	strongly disagree
1. Mrs. P has a right to expect that her wishes be respected.	❏	❏	❏	❏	❏
2. If she develops pneumonia, she should receive antibiotics.	❏	❏	❏	❏	❏
3. A physician has a right to refuse care to Mrs. P that the physician considers useless.	❏	❏	❏	❏	❏
4. If providing this care to Mrs. P would use resources that would result in care being denied to others who have hope of recovery, Mrs. P should be denied this care.	❏	❏	❏	❏	❏
5. If this care is paid for with Mrs. P's personal money, it should be provided—no matter what.	❏	❏	❏	❏	❏

INSTITUTIONAL ETHICS	strongly agree	agree	not sure	disagree	strongly disagree
1. Insurance companies would not act unethically if they refused to pay for curative care once a diagnosis of PVS is made.	❑	❑	❑	❑	❑
2. Hospitals have an ethical duty to treat patients in accord with patient wishes, whether the patient is in PVS or not.	❑	❑	❑	❑	❑
3. The hospital's decision to seek court intervention to stop useless treatment was not ethically acceptable.	❑	❑	❑	❑	❑
4. Hospitals should lobby their legislators to pass helpful legislation on questions such as these that require community clarity.	❑	❑	❑	❑	❑
5. Hospitals should develop policies that state clearly: "We provide only comfort care for persons in PVS."	❑	❑	❑	❑	❑

SOCIETAL ETHICS

	strongly agree	agree	not sure	disagree	strongly disagree
1. There should be a federal mandate requiring life-sustaining treatment for all persons who are not clearly brain dead.	❑	❑	❑	❑	❑
2. We should expand brain death laws to include those in a persistent vegetative state.	❑	❑	❑	❑	❑
3. Issues such as these are best handled by individual choice and professional judgments, not by making new laws.	❑	❑	❑	❑	❑
4. Society should conserve its resources for health care by refusing to provide more than comfort care to those in PVS.	❑	❑	❑	❑	❑
5. Medicare funds should not be used for any life-sustaining care of patients in PVS.	❑	❑	❑	❑	❑

#39: HUMAN GENOME PROJECT

The Human Genome Project is a global activity coordinated by the Human Genome Organization. Its purpose is to develop genetic maps of human chromosomes. Eventually this project intends to develop molecular maps of the estimated 3 billion base pairs of DNA of the complete human genome. The National Institute of Health in the U. S. has established the National Center for Human Genome Research (NCHGR). It works with federal, private, and international organizations to increase our understanding of the genetic aspects of human health and disease, including the prevention and treatment of the 3,000 known inherited disorders and of genetically linked physiological reactions to external factors. Over the next 15 years this U.S. commitment is expected to become the biggest U.S. investment in biomedical research ever made. The NCHGR has committed about 5% of its annual budget to research concerning ethical, legal, and social science dimensions of this effort.

INDIVIDUAL ISSUES	strongly agree	agree	not sure	disagree	strongly disagree
1. A physician should be well informed and evaluate this project critically.	❏	❏	❏	❏	❏
2. A hospital trustee has a duty to study this issue.	❏	❏	❏	❏	❏
3. A responsible physician will be politically active concerning this project.	❏	❏	❏	❏	❏
4. I should support such a program because of the care it promises future generations.	❏	❏	❏	❏	❏
5. A person suffering from genetic disease has a right to expect such community support for their health problems.	❏	❏	❏	❏	❏

INSTITUTIONAL ISSUES

	strongly agree	agree	not sure	disagree	strongly disagree
1. The AMA should strongly support this effort.	❏	❏	❏	❏	❏
2. Hospitals should engage their staffs in reflecting on the meaning of this project for our national health goals.	❏	❏	❏	❏	❏
3. Health professional societies should not simply be recipients of others' vision but should be forces helping to shape this project.	❏	❏	❏	❏	❏

	strongly agree	agree	not sure	disagree	strongly disagree

4. The press should make clear the trade-offs that will be made in pursuing this project. ❏ ❏ ❏ ❏ ❏

5. High schools/universities should engage their students in weighing the burdens and benefits of this project. ❏ ❏ ❏ ❏ ❏

SOCIETAL ISSUES

1. As a new model of global collaboration to fight disease, we should support the Genome Project wholeheartedly. ❏ ❏ ❏ ❏ ❏

2. The project has the wrong pace of investment. It should be scheduled over the next 50, not 15 years. ❏ ❏ ❏ ❏ ❏

3. A world in which 40,000 children die every day from lack of basic health care—clean water, nutrition, etc.— should give global priority to primary, not tertiary, health issues. ❏ ❏ ❏ ❏ ❏

4. The Genome Project is the crown jewel of modern preventive medicine—it deserves the support of government and public alike. ❏ ❏ ❏ ❏ ❏

5. Such an enormous project can reinforce our expectation that technology can solve all of our health problems. ❏ ❏ ❏ ❏ ❏

#40: JACK KEVORKIAN ASSISTS JONATHON GRENZ

Jonathon Grenz of Costa Mesa, California sought and received the help of Jack Kevorkian in ending his life in mid-February, 1993. He was 43 years old when he ended his life. A year before his death, he was diagnosed with throat cancer. As the disease spread, physicians surgically removed most of his tongue and implanted an electronic device on his neck to help him speak. His growing fatigue, severe impairments, and progressing illness made him withdraw more and more from contact with friends and neighbors. In a final letter to a friend he said: "I guess there's no reason to prolong any of this. I'm just not going to get any better and time goes by so slowly that it is unbearable. Life is not life any more."

INDIVIDUAL ISSUES	strongly agree	agree	not sure	disagree	strongly disagree
1. Mr. Grenz has the right to end his life when it has lost its meaning for him.	❑	❑	❑	❑	❑
2. Mr. Grenz has a right to ask others to assist in taking his life.	❑	❑	❑	❑	❑
3. Others have a duty to assist him when he so requests.	❑	❑	❑	❑	❑
4. There is no significant ethical difference between his refusing life-prolonging treatment and acting to end life.	❑	❑	❑	❑	❑
5. Persons have a right to refuse treatment, but not to ask others to kill them.	❑	❑	❑	❑	❑

INSTITUTIONAL ETHICS

	strongly agree	agree	not sure	disagree	strongly disagree
1. The state medical society should discipline a physician who assists such a request.	❑	❑	❑	❑	❑
2. The state medical society should advocate for changes in the law that would permit such assistance.	❑	❑	❑	❑	❑
3. The medical staff of a hospital should try to come to consensus on euthanasia.	❑	❑	❑	❑	❑
4. The medical staff should lobby for public policy on this issue.	❑	❑	❑	❑	❑

	strongly agree	agree	not sure	disagree	strongly disagree
5. A hospital should be active in political efforts concerning the legalization of euthanasia.	❏	❏	❏	❏	❏

SOCIETAL ETHICS

	strongly agree	agree	not sure	disagree	strongly disagree
1. An individual's right to end his/her life should be assured by law.	❏	❏	❏	❏	❏
2. Such legalization should be rejected since it establishes private killing with grave social consequences.	❏	❏	❏	❏	❏
3. Before we legalize euthanasia, we should provide adequate care for dying patients.	❏	❏	❏	❏	❏
4. What begins as empowering patients may well end in actual empowering of physicians.	❏	❏	❏	❏	❏
5. There are many options we should consider between present law and simple legalization of euthanasia.	❏	❏	❏	❏	❏

#41: PHYSICIANS CAN BUY DATA ON PATIENTS WHO HAVE SUED

Courtscan Services offers a new service to Philadelphia physicians, as of Summer, 1993. For $80 a month, they can find out whether a prospective patient has ever filed a malpractice suit against another doctor. The company has a data base of 802,000 lawsuit and judgments filed with Philadelphia's Court of Common Pleas since 1982. The service will begin in Philadelphia but will be expanded to New York, Chicago, Houston, Los Angeles and Miami within six months. The service will be expanded in other directions as well. Soon such information will be available to employers, landlords, insurers, and "others" who may be leery of litigation. This service will offer "complete litigation histories of patients in 60 seconds or less." The company's advertising counsels doctors to "screen new patients you think might be "malpractice-prone," so you can adopt necessary defensive cautionary measures." Mr. William J. Benedict, Jr., president of Courtscan Services, responded to critics that "not in a million years is a doctor going to make a decision on how to treat a patient solely on this. It's just one more piece of information. We're not making judgments for people. We're just providing information that is public."

INDIVIDUAL ISSUES	strongly agree	agree	not sure	disagree	strongly disagree
1. A physician has a right to such information.	❑	❑	❑	❑	❑
2. It is unfair that physicians can easily buy such patient information but patients cannot get equally relevant information about physicians.	❑	❑	❑	❑	❑
3. Mr. Benedict is providing a valuable service to the community.	❑	❑	❑	❑	❑
4. A physician should neither seek nor use such information because of the bias it will necessarily create.	❑	❑	❑	❑	❑
5. A physician who uses such a service has a responsibility to reveal this to all patients in his/her practice.	❑	❑	❑	❑	❑

INSTITUTIONAL ISSUES	strongly agree	agree	not sure	disagree	strongly disagree
1. Professional organizations should publicly reject such an effort.	❏	❏	❏	❏	❏
2. Health publications should carry advertising/ announcements of such a service.	❏	❏	❏	❏	❏
3. A hospital should be commended for subscribing to such a service for its own sake and that of its medical staff.	❏	❏	❏	❏	❏
4. The American Bar Association should publicly denounce such an inflammatory use of information.	❏	❏	❏	❏	❏
5. Hospitals should keep before the mind of physicians and patients that avoidance of lawsuits is grounded in excellence of communication and patient care.	❏	❏	❏	❏	❏

SOCIETAL ISSUES

	strongly agree	agree	not sure	disagree	strongly disagree
1. Such use of information should be prohibited by law.	❏	❏	❏	❏	❏
2. Courtscan should be rejected because its ultimate effect will be to intensify the litigious character of U. S. society.	❏	❏	❏	❏	❏
3. Courtscan will become more harmful as it spreads to housing, insurance, and employment fields.	❏	❏	❏	❏	❏
4. Courtscan is questionable because it is one more social empowerment for an already over-empowered group—physicians.	❏	❏	❏	❏	❏
5. There are more social benefits than burdens in the Courtscan effort.	❏	❏	❏	❏	❏

#42: PENNSYLVANIA ORGAN DONOR BILL

In March 1993, State Senator Michael Dawita of Allegheny County introduced legislation that reverses the way organs are obtained for transplantation. Under Dawita's proposal known as "presumed consent," the state would assume that a person wanted to donate one or more organs after death unless that person had obtained a non-donor card, had checked off a box against organ donation on their state income tax return or had a non-donor sticker on their driver's license. Additionally, family members would be able to veto organ donation.

Such an approach is common in Europe, a similar bill has been introduced in Maryland, and other states are reevaluating organ donor legislation. 20+ states now have partial presumed consent laws covering such "non-vital" organs as pituitary glands and corneas. But the Dawita legislation—covering vital organs—would be the first of its kind in the U.S.

INDIVIDUAL ISSUES	strongly agree	agree	not sure	disagree	strongly disagree
1. Such a law would violate my right to my own body.	❑	❑	❑	❑	❑
2. In return for all that each of us receives from the larger community, we have a duty to make our organs available to others.	❑	❑	❑	❑	❑
3. I have religious reasons to donate my organs to others.	❑	❑	❑	❑	❑
4. I should not be pressured by such a law into allowing others to violate my body.	❑	❑	❑	❑	❑
5. A person often needs a push to do what s/he sees as the right thing. This law would be such a push.	❑	❑	❑	❑	❑

INSTITUTIONAL ISSUES

	strongly agree	agree	not sure	disagree	strongly disagree
1. Hospitals should have effective systems for soliciting organs.	❑	❑	❑	❑	❑
2. Hospitals should teach staff how to effectively speak to patients/families about organ donation.	❑	❑	❑	❑	❑
3. Schools should consistently include the discussion of such issues in their educational programs.	❑	❑	❑	❑	❑

	strongly agree	agree	not sure	disagree	strongly disagree

4. Community leaders should put organ transplantation in a larger context of resource allocation. ❑ ❑ ❑ ❑ ❑

5. The media should help the public recognize that organ transplantation covers a wide range of procedures, from "routine" to extremely experimental. ❑ ❑ ❑ ❑ ❑

SOCIETAL ISSUES

1. In 1992, 29,000 people were waiting for vital organs; we need such bold social policy to meet these desperate needs. ❑ ❑ ❑ ❑ ❑

2. We should give far more emphasis to basic health care for everyone before we give increased resources to such heroic efforts for the few. ❑ ❑ ❑ ❑ ❑

3. Such a program could ultimately undermine public trust in the transplantation. It gives the impression of "organs at any price." ❑ ❑ ❑ ❑ ❑

4. It would be better to simply use some reliable market incentives to get more organs. Allowing the controlled sale of organs would solve the problem. ❑ ❑ ❑ ❑ ❑

5. Such legislation increases the over-emphasis on rescue medicine in U. S. health care. It should be opposed. ❑ ❑ ❑ ❑ ❑

#43: HOSPITAL SEEKS NOT TO TREAT ANENCEPHALIC

A suburban hospital in Virginia is appealing a federal court's ruling that it must continue to provide life-sustaining treatment for a baby born there 11 months ago. Most children with this condition die well before they reach this baby's age. An anencephalic baby has a brain stem, which sustains various vegetative functions, but lacks the higher center of the brain which is necessary for consciousness, sensation, and other cognitive functions. The mother, acting out of a "firm Christian faith that all life should be protected"—in the court's words—has insisted that everything be done to keep the baby alive. The baby is in a nursing home, but is returned to the pediatric ICU when it has periodic respiratory crises. The hospital asked for a declaration that it would not be violating any of several federal laws governing hospital admissions and discrimination against the handicapped if it refused to provide treatment the next time the baby needed it. Judge Claude M. Hilton ruled July 1, 1993 that the hospital's refusal would violate three federal laws, as well as the mother's constitutional right under the 14th Amendment's due process clause to "bring up children" in the way she thinks best.

INDIVIDUAL ISSUES	strongly agree	agree	not sure	disagree	strongly disagree
1. The mother has a right to "bring up her child" in this way.	❑	❑	❑	❑	❑
2. A physician has the right to refuse to provide life-sustaining care to this child.	❑	❑	❑	❑	❑
3. A nurse should align herself with the mother in protecting this child.	❑	❑	❑	❑	❑
4. This woman's minister should help her let her child die in peace.	❑	❑	❑	❑	❑
5. A physician would be right in using strong persuasion to change the mother's mind about treating her child.	❑	❑	❑	❑	❑

INSTITUTIONAL ISSUES					
1. The hospital is correct in taking the course it has taken.	❑	❑	❑	❑	❑
2. The hospital should defy the court order and refuse treatment.	❑	❑	❑	❑	❑

	strongly agree	agree	not sure	disagree	strongly disagree
3. The hospital should develop policies that firmly reject life-sustaining treatment for anencephalic infants.	❑	❑	❑	❑	❑
4. Insurance companies would be acting rightly if they offered policies that denied life-sustaining treatment for anencephalics.	❑	❑	❑	❑	❑
5. The nursing home should have policies against transferring such children for aggressive treatment.	❑	❑	❑	❑	❑

SOCIETAL ISSUES

	strongly agree	agree	not sure	disagree	strongly disagree
1. Eventually society should recognize anencephalic infants as brain dead.	❑	❑	❑	❑	❑
2. Society should firmly and clearly identify such children as handicapped, and insist on their strong protection.	❑	❑	❑	❑	❑
3. Society should legalize the harvesting of organs from anencephalics.	❑	❑	❑	❑	❑
4. When the U.S. has a national health program, we should provide payment for such treatment.	❑	❑	❑	❑	❑
5. Society should avoid a legislative solution to such problems and seek to use education and moral suasion.	❑	❑	❑	❑	❑

#44: LIFE SUPPORT FOR BRAIN-DEAD PREGNANT WOMAN

This much is beyond medical debate: Marion Ploch is dead. On October 4, while driving to work near the Bavarian city of Erlangen, the 18-year-old dental assistant lost control of her car and crashed. Doctors at the city's University Clinic spent the next four days trying to revive her, but the woman's injuries were too severe. She was declared legally dead on October 8. Weeks afterward, her doctors still have no intention of turning off the machines that sustain her life. Marion Ploch was 14 weeks' pregnant when she died. Somehow the crash that killed the expectant mother left the fetus unscathed. Doctors want to give the child a chance to live by sustaining the mother's life until the fetus is developed enough to survive outside the womb. Ploch never married, and the father's identity remains a mystery. At first her parents wanted to lay their daughter to rest as soon as possible, fetus or no fetus, but a prolonged reflection convinced them to support this attempt to save the fetus. Eventually they appeared on national TV and vowed to raise the child as their own (they are in their mid-30s). "We will do everything we can to see that when our baby is born, it gets all the love it can." Doctors have succeeded before in maintaining brain-dead pregnant women until their fetuses became viable.

INDIVIDUAL ISSUES	strongly agree	agree	not sure	disagree	strongly disagree
1. Ms. Ploch is dead and this is the main issue. Treatment should be stopped.	❏	❏	❏	❏	❏
2. The fetus can be saved and that is the main issue. Treatment should be continued.	❏	❏	❏	❏	❏
3. The wishes of Ms. Ploch, if known, should determine what we do.	❏	❏	❏	❏	❏
4. To allow the fetus to die would be tragic but not unethical.	❏	❏	❏	❏	❏
5. Ms. Ploch's parents, as her surrogates, should have the power to decide about her continued treatment.	❏	❏	❏	❏	❏

INSTITUTIONAL ISSUES

	strongly agree	agree	not sure	disagree	strongly disagree
1. It would be ethically justified if the clinic had a policy of not providing life-sustaining treatment in such cases.	❏	❏	❏	❏	❏
2. There should be professional guidelines to guide physicians in making such decisions.	❏	❏	❏	❏	❏
3. An insurance company should not have to pay for such heroic care.	❏	❏	❏	❏	❏
4. Churches should develop guidelines for their believers to follow in such cases.	❏	❏	❏	❏	❏
5. Schools should promote consideration of such questions as part of standard education.	❏	❏	❏	❏	❏

SOCIETAL ISSUES

	strongly agree	agree	not sure	disagree	strongly disagree
1. The resources used in this attempt (possibly over $500,000) will result in care being denied to others with a better chance at survival. So much money for so little chance cannot be ethically justified.	❏	❏	❏	❏	❏
2. Society should support such protection of fetal life.	❏	❏	❏	❏	❏
3. Society should resist the consideration of money in such a case.	❏	❏	❏	❏	❏
4. We should spend more resources on long-term health care rather than on such marginally beneficial care.	❏	❏	❏	❏	❏
5. Society should always be able to find the resources to provide care in such tragic cases.	❏	❏	❏	❏	❏

#45: GAY MARRIAGE

Hawaii's highest court has taken an important step toward making the state the first in the country to recognize marriages between couples of the same sex. The high court ruled that Hawaii's ban on such marriages may violate the State Constitution's prohibition against sex discrimination. The majority opinion stated that "marriage is a basic civil right," and that "on its face and as applied," the current Hawaii law "denies same-sex couples access to the marital status and concomitant rights and benefits." If Hawaii moves forward in recognizing same-sex marriages, it will have nationwide consequences.

All states in the U.S. recognize marriages performed in other states. So, unless the other states change this practice, gay couples married in Hawaii will have to be recognized as married couples in other states, entitling them to tax breaks, health and survivor benefits that accrue to married partners.

There is a growing recognition that gay couples constitute families. In the last 10 years about 30 municipalities, including New York and San Francisco, have adopted policies recognizing gay couples as "domestic partners," and granting them limited benefits.

INDIVIDUAL ISSUES	strongly agree	agree	not sure	disagree	strongly disagree
1. Those who choose a homosexual lifestyle must be prepared to accept current U.S. social consequences.	❏	❏	❏	❏	❏
2. Homosexuality is not a choice, and social policy should not discriminate against natural conditions.	❏	❏	❏	❏	❏
3. The underlying reality of marriage is a commitment to share life, which is relevant to couples of various sexual orientations.	❏	❏	❏	❏	❏
4. Any adults who want to enter marriage have the right to do so, and laws should reflect this right.	❏	❏	❏	❏	❏
5. Objections to homosexual marriage probably have homophobia as part of their basis.	❏	❏	❏	❏	❏

INSTITUTIONAL ISSUES

	strongly agree	agree	not sure	disagree	strongly disagree
1. Schools should help children be accepting of homosexual marriages.	❏	❏	❏	❏	❏
2. Schools should strongly emphasize the ideal of heterosexuality.	❏	❏	❏	❏	❏
3. Mental health professionals should help dismantle homophobic rejection of gay marriage.	❏	❏	❏	❏	❏
4. TV should treat the theme of same-sex marriage more extensively.	❏	❏	❏	❏	❏
5. Religious groups would be correct in lobbying against the legalization of gay marriage.	❏	❏	❏	❏	❏

SOCIETAL ISSUES

	strongly agree	agree	not sure	disagree	strongly disagree
1. There are strong social reasons for rejecting gay marriage.	❏	❏	❏	❏	❏
2. Hawaii would show leadership in moving forward in eventually legalizing gay marriage.	❏	❏	❏	❏	❏
3. If Hawaii legalizes gay marriage, other states should stand firm in the rejection.	❏	❏	❏	❏	❏
4. My state should recognize gay couples as "domestic partners" for some rights and benefits, but not for all marital rights and benefits.	❏	❏	❏	❏	❏
5. My states should grant full marital rights and benefits to gay couples seeking marriage.	❏	❏	❏	❏	❏

#46: TELEVISION VIOLENCE

Brandon Centerwall, an epidemiologist at the University of Washington, studied the relationship between TV violence and the growth of violence in various communities. His conclusion: TV violence is a public health problem deserving measures as practical as nutrition, immunization and bicycle helmet programs. He cites such studies as one from a remote Canadian community that in 1973 was due to acquire television. Social scientists seized the opportunity to investigate the effects of television on this community's children, using for comparison two similar towns that had long had television. Before television arrived, they monitored rates of inappropriate physical aggression among 45 first- and second-graders. After two years of television, the rate increased 160%, in both boys and girls, and in those who were aggressive to begin with and those who were not. The rate in the two communities that had television for years did not change. Centerwall believes that the television industry is as unlikely to attend to such issues as is the tobacco industry to attend to the link between smoking and cancer. Therefore, he concludes, we need to find other ways to deal with this powerful source of violence in our communities.

INDIVIDUAL ISSUES	strongly agree	agree	not sure	disagree	strongly disagree
1. Without a proven link between violence and TV, we are not justified in attempts to control TV violence.	❑	❑	❑	❑	❑
2. I have a right to watch what I want on TV.	❑	❑	❑	❑	❑
3. Parents should monitor what children watch— there is no other solution.	❑	❑	❑	❑	❑
4. TV is part of my "neighborhood," and I have some rights about what goes on in this space I share with my neighbors.	❑	❑	❑	❑	❑
5. If you don't like what's on TV, don't buy a TV set. But don't put your morality on me.	❑	❑	❑	❑	❑

INSTITUTIONAL ISSUES

	strongly agree	agree	not sure	disagree	strongly disagree
1. Educators should lobby for limiting violence on TV.	❑	❑	❑	❑	❑
2. Schools should make critical viewing of television a consistent part of the educational process.	❑	❑	❑	❑	❑

	strongly agree	agree	not sure	disagree	strongly disagree

3. Health professionals should identify TV violence as a widespread health hazard, and target this problem as they do other health dangers. ❑ ❑ ❑ ❑ ❑

4. Churches should organize their communities to take political action against TV violence. ❑ ❑ ❑ ❑ ❑

5. Churches should organize boycotts against advertisers who promote TV violence. ❑ ❑ ❑ ❑ ❑

SOCIETAL ISSUES

1. Society is justified in taking strong steps against infectious diseases; TV violence also warrants such strong steps. ❑ ❑ ❑ ❑ ❑

2. Any attempts to limit the content of TV are censorship. In our society such censorship should be rejected. ❑ ❑ ❑ ❑ ❑

3. We should develop a "sin tax" that is levied for every act of violence on a TV program. ❑ ❑ ❑ ❑ ❑

4. We should recognize TV as the single most powerful educational institution in the U.S., and treat it accordingly. ❑ ❑ ❑ ❑ ❑

5. In our society, television is essentially a marketable item. We should not change that orientation. ❑ ❑ ❑ ❑ ❑

#47: 3-D PICTURES OF THE HEART WITHOUT SURGERY

A new technique—echo-CT—allows us to view inside the beating heart without cutting it open. A new generation of machines—a technological marriage of ultrasound and CT scanners—produces three-dimensional pictures that look like ordinary movies. Doctors can simulate slicing through the heart at any angle, then peek inside and watch valves flap and chamber walls pulse. The startlingly sharp pictures look as though a miniature video camera had somehow been threaded into the heart and turned on.

Advocates say that the technology's most promising advantage is giving surgeons an advance look at what they will see when they operate. Such a perspective offers substantial advantages for the outcome of surgery. Critics are concerned that the improved diagnostic advantage is bought at a disproportionately high cost.

INDIVIDUAL ISSUES	strongly agree	agree	not sure	disagree	strongly disagree
1. Individuals in such dire need have a right to this care.	❑	❑	❑	❑	❑
2. It would be cruel to deny this treatment to someone who could benefit from it.	❑	❑	❑	❑	❑
3. If I can pay for it, I should be able to get such care.	❑	❑	❑	❑	❑
4. It would be unjust to deny a surgeon access to such a clinical advantage.	❑	❑	❑	❑	❑
5. Where life is concerned, we should not talk money.	❑	❑	❑	❑	❑

INSTITUTIONAL ISSUES					
1. The AMA should press for the funding of such technology.	❑	❑	❑	❑	❑
2. Insurance companies could rightly deny payment for such treatment.	❑	❑	❑	❑	❑
3. A quality hospital will provide such treatment as soon as possible.	❑	❑	❑	❑	❑
4. Labor unions should insist on coverage for such treatment when it is available.	❑	❑	❑	❑	❑

	strongly agree	agree	not sure	disagree	strongly disagree
5. Hospitals should develop guidelines to prevent the overuse of such an expensive technology.	❏	❏	❏	❏	❏

SOCIETAL ISSUES

	strongly agree	agree	not sure	disagree	strongly disagree
1. Society should limit such development in light of an overall set of health priorities.	❏	❏	❏	❏	❏
2. Society should see to it that the entrepreneurial spirit of America is the only limit set to such ventures.	❏	❏	❏	❏	❏
3. Federal guidelines should steer funds away from this to basic care.	❏	❏	❏	❏	❏
4. Since it is difficult to limit the use of such technology, once developed, we need to slow the development of such treatments.	❏	❏	❏	❏	❏
5. Society should provide no public moneys for such research until all children are vaccinated.	❏	❏	❏	❏	❏

#48: DEATH PENALTY

For 10 years the United States experienced a moratorium on capital punishment. In 1977 we reinstituted the death penalty. This was, in part, a response to the rise in violent crime which continues to escalate:

> 1983 1.25 million violent crimes/19,310 murders
> 1990 1.80 million violent crimes/23,440 murders.

In our history we have executed roughly 18,000 persons. 180 of these executions have occurred since the reintroduction of the death penalty in 1977.

In July 1992, the Catholic Bishops' Conference of the Philippines issued a statement: "Restoring the Death Penalty: A Backward Step." In this document they reject the death penalty on three grounds: 1) they judge the death penalty to be an attack on the dignity of all life; 2) they note that the poor are de facto disproportionately the victims of the death penalty; 3) there is no demonstrated data that the death penalty serves the common good as a deterrent.

INDIVIDUAL ISSUES	strongly agree	agree	not sure	disagree	strongly disagree
1. I favor the reinstitution of the death penalty.	❑	❑	❑	❑	❑
2. The death penalty is justified because taking the criminal's life vindicates the crime.	❑	❑	❑	❑	❑
3. The death penalty is valid because some persons are beyond rehabilitation.	❑	❑	❑	❑	❑
4. The death penalty fits some crimes because the criminal has lost the right to life by committing the crime.	❑	❑	❑	❑	❑
5. The death penalty harms individual citizens by fostering their vindictiveness.	❑	❑	❑	❑	❑

INSTITUTIONAL ISSUES

	strongly agree	agree	not sure	disagree	strongly disagree
1. The media should help educate the public about the realities of the death penalty.	❑	❑	❑	❑	❑
2. Schools should do more to educate students about crime and punishment.	❑	❑	❑	❑	❑
3. Churches should help their communities see the religious relevance of the issue of capital punishment.	❑	❑	❑	❑	❑

	strongly agree	agree	not sure	disagree	strongly disagree

4. Mental health professionals should help the public better understand some of the key psychological elements of crime and punishment. ❑ ❑ ❑ ❑ ❑

5. Physicians, as professionals dedicated to preserving life, should lobby to abolish the death penalty. ❑ ❑ ❑ ❑ ❑

SOCIETAL ISSUES

1. The Supreme Court was correct in reinstating the possibility of the death penalty in 1977. ❑ ❑ ❑ ❑ ❑

2. Society should deal with deep sources of violence—poverty, racism, family decay, etc.,—as a more constructive way to resolve violent behavior, rather than reacting with the death penalty. ❑ ❑ ❑ ❑ ❑

3. Actual practice of the death penalty is wrong because it operates as one more mechanism of the structural racism of U. S. society. ❑ ❑ ❑ ❑ ❑

4. We should allow capital punishment, but only for the most heinous and violent crimes. ❑ ❑ ❑ ❑ ❑

5. Society owes the residents of death row rehabilitation, not execution, since virtually all of them were victims of sustained and severe abuse as children. ❑ ❑ ❑ ❑ ❑

#49: OUTCOMES "REPORT CARDS"

In January 1993, 10 major companies asked that any health reform package include a data-collecting mechanism that could issue report cards for quality, including measures specifically targeting rates of preventive services, management of chronic conditions, effectiveness of prenatal care, health status and changes in outcome and patient satisfaction. If individuals and corporations are going to become more informed consumers and purchasers of health care, they will need solid information. Dr. Stephen Schoenbaum, deputy medical director of Harvard Community Health Plan, says that outcomes measurement is absolutely necessary. But he also emphasizes that such an approach is in its infancy. "We do believe a lot of the care we deliver is inappropriate care or unnecessary care. We don't have good outcomes data. We substitute our beliefs about outcomes for knowledge."

There is both strong support for such report card efforts and strong resistance.

INDIVIDUAL ISSUES	strongly agree	agree	not sure	disagree	strongly disagree
1. Patients have right to know such data.	❑	❑	❑	❑	❑
2. Such data provides a basis for genuine informed consent.	❑	❑	❑	❑	❑
3. Such data can be easily misunderstood and lead to an erroneous and harmful impact on health care providers.	❑	❑	❑	❑	❑
4. Such data will probably put more money into the spin doctors' pockets than knowledge into the consumers' minds.	❑	❑	❑	❑	❑
5. A physician should welcome such initiative on the part of patients to join in quality care.	❑	❑	❑	❑	❑

INSTITUTIONAL ISSUES

	strongly agree	agree	not sure	disagree	strongly disagree
1. Hospitals should promote the careful gathering of such data.	❑	❑	❑	❑	❑
2. Hospitals have every right to use favorable outcome data—when available—as a marketing tool.	❑	❑	❑	❑	❑

	strongly agree	*agree*	*not sure*	*disagree*	*strongly disagree*
3. Beyond patient satisfaction, hospitals should invest effort in evaluating the *appropriateness* of care in their institution.	❑	❑	❑	❑	❑
4. Managed care efforts are driven almost exclusively by economics.	❑	❑	❑	❑	❑
5. Professional organizations should promote the careful use of such data for the good of patients.	❑	❑	❑	❑	❑

SOCIETAL ISSUES

	strongly agree	*agree*	*not sure*	*disagree*	*strongly disagree*
1. This field is too immature to serve the common good at this time.	❑	❑	❑	❑	❑
2. We should begin using such data, recognizing its shortcomings, but learn by doing.	❑	❑	❑	❑	❑
3. Taking such an approach reinforces the mistaken notion that health care is a consumer good.	❑	❑	❑	❑	❑
4. Such data is best gathered and used by professional groups, not by the naive public.	❑	❑	❑	❑	❑
5. Since peer review has been so ineffective in overseeing the quality of health care, it is better to give full disclosure to the general public.	❑	❑	❑	❑	❑

#50: TOBACCO

In 1993, a 40-year study of British doctors revealed some very bad news for smokers. This study was conducted by the Imperial Cancer Research Center at Oxford University. The study followed 34,439 male doctors for 40 years, offering some of the earliest evidence linking smoking and lung cancer. The new results are much more extreme than had been suggested by the 20-year follow-up. At that point, premature death was only twice as common in smokers as in nonsmokers. Of participants between age 44 and 70, 1.69% of smokers died annually, compared with 0.57% of non-smokers. In the 45-54 age group, 1.14% of smokers died each year, compared with 0.38% of nonsmokers. For those 55 to 64, 2.25% of smokers died, compared with 0.77% of nonsmokers. Such news should weigh heavily on American taxpayers, who annually provide over $100 million in taxpayer help for the tobacco industry.

INDIVIDUAL ISSUES	strongly agree	agree	not sure	disagree	strongly disagree
1. There are many risky behaviors—eating, drinking, driving, recreating—and individuals have a right to live at their own level of risk.	❏	❏	❏	❏	❏
2. The data on smoking is so conclusive that persons have a responsibility to stop smoking.	❏	❏	❏	❏	❏
3. Parents have a duty to stop smoking for the sake of their children.	❏	❏	❏	❏	❏
4. A public figure should not smoke as a good example for society—especially for children.	❏	❏	❏	❏	❏
5. Smoking is an addiction and should not be treated as if it were freely chosen behavior.	❏	❏	❏	❏	❏

INSTITUTIONAL ISSUES					
1. Schools should prohibit all smoking on school property.	❏	❏	❏	❏	❏
2. Businesses should make their facilities smoke-free.	❏	❏	❏	❏	❏
3. Insurance companies should provide maximum incentives to stop smoking among their policy-holders.	❏	❏	❏	❏	❏
4. Merchants should refuse to sell candy cigarettes.	❏	❏	❏	❏	❏

5. Since smoking correlates to socio/economic/ educational status, organizations should be cautious about applying sanctions for its practice.

	strongly agree	agree	not sure	disagree	strongly disagree
	❑	❑	❑	❑	❑

SOCIETAL ISSUES

1. Tobacco advertising in all forms should be outlawed.

	strongly agree	agree	not sure	disagree	strongly disagree
	❑	❑	❑	❑	❑

2. Education—not law—should be the major social tactic in stopping tobacco use.

| | ❑ | ❑ | ❑ | ❑ | ❑ |

3. Tobacco taxes should be at least several dollars a pack.

| | ❑ | ❑ | ❑ | ❑ | ❑ |

4. It is a moral outrage that government supports the success of the tobacco enterprise.

| | ❑ | ❑ | ❑ | ❑ | ❑ |

5. Our society should make smoking tobacco as illegal as smoking pot.

| | ❑ | ❑ | ❑ | ❑ | ❑ |

#51: EMBRYOSCOPY: WINDOW INTO THE WOMB

Definitions on three levels: one of the steps in doing the full range of ethics concerning an issue is to try to define/describe the issue on three levels. The following offers some examples of such multi-leveled definition/description.

At Wayne State University's Hutzel Hospital, doctors are utilizing a miniature scope inserted into the womb through a needle the size of one used to draw blood. This is remarkably smaller than any scope available up to now. With the new amazing optics, doctors can examine the embryo as closely as if the woman's womb were opened. Embryoscopy, as the new technology is called, is poised to become an invaluable tool in diagnosing abnormalities of embryos and fetuses far earlier and more precisely than ever before. Abnormalities can now be detected at nine weeks that could only be detected at 19 weeks with older technologies, such as ultrasound. Other abnormalities can be seen that could not be detected with amniocentesis or chorionic villus sampling. Pregnant women can also be reassured that their fetus is completely normal, even though there might have been suspicious shadows on ultrasound or a frightening genetic history. This same technology now puts fetal surgery and therapy on the horizon. Dr. Pergament of Northwestern University says: "It's a question of who's going to be the first one to do it."

DEFINITIONS/DESCRIPTIONS ON INDIVIDUAL LEVEL

- a new possibility to know about fetal health;

- a new possibility to provide peace and security to parents;

- a new possibility for more accurate diagnosis;

- a new possibility for earlier diagnosis;

- a new possibility for diagnosis of currently undiagnosable abnormalities;

- a new method to deliver therapy at the earliest possible opportunity;

- provides physicians with a powerful diagnostic tool.

DEFINITIONS/DESCRIPTIONS ON INSTITUTIONAL LEVEL

- new patient service;

- new source of revenue;

- opportunity to recruit physicians;

- new risk/liability issue;

- new marketing reality—the mark of a cutting-edge institution;

- need for education of staff;

- institutional trade-offs/opportunity costs.

DEFINITIONS/DESCRIPTIONS ON SOCIETAL LEVEL

- create greater expectations in public for diagnostic miracles;

- create expectations for fetal surgery;

- earlier chance to make choice about abortion;

- increased allocation of health dollars for diagnosis/treatment;

- pressure for funds away from prevention and long-term care;

- more hope in medical technology to solve problems;

- further empowerment of physicians.